HAPPINESS
HABITS

The Urban Professional's Guide to Good Living

*A life-changing approach to finding
lasting joy and fulfilment*

Sriram S

INDIA · SINGAPORE · MALAYSIA

Notion Press Media Pvt Ltd

No. 50, Chettiyar Agaram Main Road,
Vanagaram, Chennai, Tamil Nadu – 600 095

First Published by Notion Press 2021
Copyright © Sriram S 2021
All Rights Reserved.

ISBN 978-1-68586-738-6

To my grandmother, Savitri, without whom I would not be the person I am.

Contents

Acknowledgements

Writing this book was long due and the next step in my journey towards my purpose. A lot of people have supported this endeavour and I would like to acknowledge their contribution in making this happen.

First and foremost, the Divine because, without divine synchronicities, this book would not have been possible.

I would like to acknowledge my late grandmother Savitri for giving me all that I needed to live a good life.

I would like to thank Supriya Jain, Juveria Samrin, and Nitin Sisupalan for being the driving force behind the book. I thank my wife Latha and my daughters, Anannya and Kimaya, for inspiring me and teaching me the things I needed to know to be able to write this book. I would also like to thank my uncle Velanand, my aunts Tulsi and Sumi, my parents, my sister, and my cousins for their support.

I would like to acknowledge Rachel, Rhishi, and Vishal for their help with the content and my friend Madhavan Palanisamy for his photography and encouragement. A heartfelt thank you to my coaches—Harrish Sairaman, Sheila Mathilakath, Mamatha Vuttaradi, and Manisha Nihalanii—for their constant encouragement and direction. I would also like to acknowledge the many teachers who have all helped me evolve as a human and given me the capability to guide others.

Last but not the least I would like to acknowledge all the companies and the people that I have worked with—Infosys, DE Shaw India, and Arcesium India—for their belief in my capabilities.

The Day I Died

June 7th, for the unconcerned observer, dawned like any other summer day. It was also the day I died and came back to life!

I still remember, it was a Saturday. I woke up in a weekend mindset—just a few things to do before I wind up for the week and relax. I had barely brushed my teeth before the phone rang. It was my aunt Sumi.

I picked up the phone, and the first thing I registered was how distraught she sounded.

'Ram… Ram. He died. Eku is dead!'

'What!' That was all my shocked brain could think of. He was such a hale and hearty man in good health. I couldn't comprehend him dying!

'Ram, Tulsi just called me. He had a heart attack. She is beside herself. Anand and Vikram are too far away. Please go to her. She needs you,' my aunt's entreaties came from the other end.

'Yes… I'll be there. I'm booking my tickets right now,' I managed to reply, though my mind was a whirlwind of thoughts and emotions.

I was very close to my aunt Tulsi. As a child I had spent many summer holidays with her and my cousins—blissfully happy as only a child can be. Growing up and attending to the demands of a career had limited our interactions but not our love.

I walked out of my room quite mechanically and told my wife what had happened and that I was heading to Chennai. I booked my tickets for the first flight out and called an Uber to the airport. Once the check-in formalities were done, I sat down to wait for my flight to be called. I tried reading a book, but I just couldn't concentrate. My mind wandered back to the wonderful man who was my uncle and how devastated my aunt must be feeling now.

The last I spoke to my uncle; he was admonishing me for my rapidly deteriorating lifestyle.

'Ram, you need to take better care of yourself. You are a young man; you have small children. If you don't take care of yourself, how will you take care of them?' My uncle had boomed in his loud voice.

I had adopted the lifestyle that's the trademark of most urban working professionals today. I worked long hours, ate junk food, indulged in binge drinking, and had irregular sleep patterns. And it was showing. I was irritable, had perpetual headaches, and was putting on weight. Hence, my uncle's concern.

'Yes Uncle, I will.' I told him, with no intention of following through on it. After all, when there is so much to do, who has time for self-care!

'You take care of yourself and aunty. I'll talk to you soon.' These were my last words to him. And now we'll never speak again.

I couldn't help the sadness that engulfed me, and with a heavy heart, I boarded the flight. The flight was short, but I couldn't relax. My uncle's unexpected death had given me the stark realization of the frailty of life.

As soon as I arrived at my aunt's place I was sucked into the logistics. We had to wait for my cousins to arrive from abroad to cremate the body. I tried consoling my aunt—seeing her in such a distraught state was extremely difficult for me.

As time passed, many of the mourners had left and I settled in the room next to the one where my uncle had passed away. I had been feeling a discomfort in my chest since afternoon but dismissed it. There was no time to pay attention to it and I thought the emotional turmoil had resulted in the pain. I was also feeling a bit weak and light-headed but chalked it up to the meals that I skipped throughout the day. But by evening, with time to think and reflect, I felt the pain getting worse.

I tried sleeping. I didn't want to bother anyone or create a fuss. But I couldn't do more than toss and turn. Every time I closed my eyes, I had strange visions.

My uncle's death had rattled me, and I couldn't stop thinking about what was happening to me.

'What if it's a heart attack?'

'What if I am dying right now, far away from my wife and kids?'

'My youngest daughter was only a month old; I couldn't die on her!'

Even as I thought along these lines, the tightness in my chest got progressively worse. Soon, I felt like I could not breathe. I had to get some help!

I got hold of another cousin who was staying at my aunt's house and informed him about my symptoms. He immediately urged me to go with him to a hospital. We reached a hospital nearby; but it was ill-equipped. A technician was sitting in a dimly lit basement with the ECG equipment next to a bed that had seen better days. There was no air conditioning to provide relief from a hot Indian summer. I lay down on the dirty sheet and he—quite amateurishly—plugged in the probes.

The pain and discomfort, the shabby experience, and the fumbling attempts of the technician resulted in an irregular ECG. They asked me to get admitted immediately. By then, my belief in the competence of the hospital staff was shaken. So, my cousin and I decided to move me to another hospital a bit farther away but with better facilities. I was already exhausted—mentally and physically—from the day, and the delay did not really help my mental state. I was convinced I was dying and would not see the sunrise tomorrow.

It's funny what the thought of death does to a person.

I was in my thirties, and this was the first time I had come face-to-face with my own mortality.

Honestly, I was scared.

I didn't want to die.

I had so much that I still needed to get done… So much that I wanted to experience!

I wanted to spend more time with my loved ones. I wanted to see my children grow up. I wanted to do things that I was passionate about.

The midnight dash to emergency rooms was surreal—my life flashing before my eyes. Even as my cousin rushed me to the next hospital, I was busy praying and making promises to God.

I would change my lifestyle.

I would live better.

I would live consciously.

I would value my life, if given another chance.

As it happened, I *was* given another chance. And so, I am here, sharing my story, and taking this moment to talk to you about LIFE.

This episode taught me that we find a new appreciation of life when we have seen death looming close by. But not all of us are given a second lease of life. I count myself lucky—in more ways than one.

This brush with death was the beginning of my new life.

Suddenly, living a better, more wholesome life, had become more serious, more urgent.

I wanted to honour the promises I made to myself, and to God, in the frantic hours of that night on 7 Jun 2014.

So, I started on this journey to be a better version of myself, to be happier. I tried many things. I went through several healing modalities like hypnotherapy, tapping, Reiki, etc. I learned from the top teachers in self-development both from the Western and Eastern philosophies. When I listened to some of the gurus, it seemed like an impossible proposition to become like them. They were so far away from the life we live today that what worked for them couldn't possibly work for me. And I didn't want to give up everything! My pursuit was just about discovering a better place within my everyday life.

And I realized something. ***Happiness isn't a grand shift that happens overnight. It's a state that you achieve after making small adjustments and creating new habits over time.***

It's been over seven years since I started down this road of transformation, and I have learnt many things. I managed to turn my life around!

I stopped drinking.

I started caring for myself and my wellbeing.

I learnt how to live with flow.

I was still the same person, I was still doing the same job, but I was living a fuller life. If you asked me how that happened, I'd attribute it to a mindset shift.

There was a shift in my perspective of life, there was a shift in my behaviour, and all this was because there was a fundamental shift in how I thought.

For someone who was paranoid and driven by fear, I was able to slowly shift from that to being an optimist. I was happier, I was less worried, I was doing more of the things I enjoyed.

I had somehow cracked a bit of the code and figured out some of the ingredients of a happier life within the construct of the modern urban lifestyle.

This was exciting!

Changing my life didn't need any special gifts or superpowers. It didn't require drastic action, rather a gradual metamorphosis through consistent action. It meant that if I—a typical, materialistic, common man—could do it, then anyone could do it.

And so, I decided to write this book. Happiness Habits is intended to be the urban professional guide to a happier life.

I'm NOT going to ask you to give up everything and become a monk.

I'm NOT going to give you any quick fixes or zero-effort transformations.

I'm NOT going to preach to you.

The intent of this book is to make you aware of the possibility that's within the grasp of each of us and to give you actionable steps to attain it.

If you've got your hands on this book, you are already seeking happiness. You know that there is a missing piece, and you want to find it. You know your life can be so much better and you are ready to change it. You've already opened up and asked the universe for help… and it has delivered this book to you.

In this book, I will take you through a step-by-step framework that will help you become more aware of what happiness means to you. I'll show you the science behind my suggestions and follow it up with a solid way to practise and implement them.

What I'm presenting to you in this book has been tried and tested. I started a personal development club called LEAP—Limitless Excellence and Accelerated Performance—in 2016 and, over the years, have trained people on personal development techniques ranging from Visualisation, Meditation, Mindfulness, Gratitude, Intuition, etc. I have also done several workshops for academic institutions, including IIMs and IITs, as well as industry bodies like NHRD on these topics. This book distils all my learnings in this journey and packs it up in a Happiness Habits bundle for you.

My attempt in this book is to keep it real, keep it in the realm of possibility, and make it worth your time.

And I don't want you to take my word for it. Don't believe everything I say! Take it for what it is: 'a possibility', and do your own experimenting and see what it shifts for you.

Onwards in the pursuit of happiness…

How to Use This Book

The intent of the book is to help you answer some questions for yourself.

- What really makes me happy?
- What can I change to make happiness a part of my everyday life?
- How do I go about making these changes?
- What can I do to make sure these changes will stick?
- What can I do if I fall off the plan?

While this book is about understanding happiness, it's a lot about embodying it in your everyday life. As you read this book, I'd encourage you to go chapter by chapter and make use of the reflection exercises at the end of each chapter. These reflection exercises are designed to help you **discover** what you need to do, **decide** what you want to do, and **strategize** on how you want to do it. As you move through the book, reflecting on each section, it'll uncover the **blueprint of your happiness**. You can use the space in the book itself to note down your thoughts and actions or create a separate notebook to jot down your plan of action.

This book also comes with tons of bonus content that is available online at *www.happinesshabits.in* absolutely FREE. All you need to do to access it is to scan the QR code inside this book and create your unique login ID.

Happiness Decoded

Happiness cannot be travelled to, owned, earned, worn, or consumed. Happiness is the spiritual experience of living every minute with love, grace, and gratitude.

– Denis Waitley

Myths of Happiness

For a while after my uncle's death, I couldn't sleep well. I was plagued with strange dreams that I couldn't make sense of. All I could see was fog, but I knew there was something waiting for me under it all. But try as I might I was not able to dispel the fog.

And suddenly one night, expecting foggy dreams, I found myself surrounded by pitch dark instead. It was a strange place that was eerily quiet and smelled quite musty. Like a place taking its last breaths. I looked around, trying to find a speck of light, and found some flashes coming from a distance. On. Off. On. Off... and so they went. I started walking towards them and found myself in some sort of a jungle. There were vines all around me. But wait, they looked like cables!

A fast-moving ball of light streaked past me like a bullet train— and then it was dark again. I kept moving and came across gleaming spider-webs. Or are they neurons?

What kind of a place is this? What is going on here?

AM I INSIDE MY BRAIN?!

WHY am I here?

And what's that noise?

I strained my eyes to peer through the still dark landscape. In the purple shadows all around me and the light show from the firing neurons and I could make out a shape perched high on the branches of a cable-tree. It looked like a bird. Wait, it looked like a raven.

What's a raven doing in my head?

I was feeling a bit like Alice in Wonderland. Maybe I should wake up now. But I had no clue how to do that. The only thing I knew for sure was that there was nothing in my warm drink before bed that would give me these visions.

After standing around for a while, and not being able to make much sense of it all, I finally decided to ask the bird. Umm… yeah. I was going to talk to a bird! Sue me!

I cleared my throat—and in a voice that said I speak to birds on a regular basis—I asked, 'Who are you? Where are we? And what are you doing here?'

'Woah, too many questions, my friend,' said the raven.

Surprise, surprise! The raven talks! Of course.

'Well, answer me.'

'Aren't you an impatient one,' snarked the raven. 'I am your spirit guide, Siddha—the wise one of old. Call me Sid.'

That threw me for a toss! 'Guide? I don't need a guide! And why would YOU be my guide? What could you possibly guide me on!'

'There he goes with the questions again,' muttered… Sid. Then a little louder he said, 'One word… HAPPINESS.'

Seeing me shocked, he continued, 'I know you have been searching for happiness. I know you have been asking how you can be happy most of the time. And I am here to show you the answer. In fact, I'll show you something right now, and then you can decide if I am good enough to be your guide or not.'

That got my attention. 'Well, what are you waiting for? Do your thing. Show me.' I replied.

'So much attitude! And then he wonders why he's unhappy.' I swear I could see Sid roll his eyes.

'Hey!' I protested. 'That was mean. Aren't you wise ones supposed to be goody-goody?'

All I got for that was another eye roll before Sid hopped on ahead and pointed to a dense cluster of cables and sockets.

'Do you see that mess?' he asked. I nodded to indicate I did.

'Take a closer look. Can you see anything else?'

I went closer and squinted at the cables snaking around everywhere and sockets mounted on walls. There seemed to be some writing on the sockets. Ah. 'Relationships,' I read out. 'Work, health, money, here's another one… parenting, spirituality, anxiety,' I rattled on.

I looked up at Sid and asked, 'what's the meaning of this?'

If ravens could smirk, I am sure Sid did! 'This, my boy, is your salvation. Your key to happiness,' he crowed. 'You see, your life is a mess as we can see here, and we are going to sort it out.'

At my blank stare, he sighed and pointed to the socket that read 'anxiety'. 'Unplug that cable there and plug it into the socket that says 'meditation',' he commanded.

I did that. And soon I was unplugging toxic relationships and plugging into appreciation. I was unplugging emotional eating and plugging into wellbeing. And as I unplugged and plugged into new stuff, I started seeing some new pathways getting created. The cables were also looking so much more organized now!

Sid then took me to what looked like a dump-yard of software code. Here I was given more instructions that changed the code. We walked further… well he flew, and I walked. Some sort of a storage system was waiting for us. He directed me to the memory discs, and I had to pull out a few and delete them. This was getting tiring now and I was still not clear on what we were trying to do.

Just as I was about to give up, I found myself surrounded in brilliance. All this work that I had done had removed blocks and created new pathways. And these pathways were now shining a bright fluorescent green, taking away the darkness and bathing us in light.

It felt like the whole landscape had just come alive. Where there was darkness, it was now light. Where there was an eerie silence there was now a soothing sound. Where there was a musty, old smell, there was a pleasant aroma wafting in the air.

As I was taking it all in, I felt the raven settle down on my shoulder. He rubbed his beak on my head and, almost gently, said, 'It's all in your head you fool! You can choose to rewire and recode yourself for happiness. You can release the memories of the past that are keeping you stuck. You can frame new beliefs and new thoughts that will result in new behaviours and lead you to happiness.'

Then he looked at me sternly, 'but for this, you have to do the work. Work on yourself, practise happiness through your habits, and you will learn to become a better human and a happier person.'

I was just registering these words when Sid faded away. The light seemed even brighter, and colours danced in front of my eyelids. The landscape vanished too. I was waking up!

I couldn't believe it was a dream. It felt so 'present'. I could still feel the energy of the transformed landscape. The momentary bliss I had experienced towards the end. And unlike dreams that one forgets, this one was staying with me. I knew it meant something important.

But even as I was thinking about Sid the raven, another voice popped up. Looked like I wasn't done with the voices in my head! This one sounded more like my pessimistic self—dripping with scorn and disbelief.

'What utter rubbish,' it said. 'Who in their right minds gives any importance to dreams? You've lost it!'

'Right, just what I needed. Another weird voice in my head. I'm sure this one will cook up a name too!' I thought.

'Too right! I am Neuro. Your anchor to reality and your saviour from flights of fancy and dreamland induced idiocy.' It piped up again.

'What's the harm in analysing a dream?' I asked. 'It was a new perspective. An interesting one. Maybe it's just what I need! I think what Sid was trying to tell me was that happiness is a choice and that I need to rewire myself from within rather than look for it outside. I think that makes sense!'

'So, are you saying that billions of people, chasing happiness in fame, success, beauty, money, etc. are all wrong?' Neuro butted in.

'No, but it does merit thought, doesn't it? Are these people happy?' I countered.

There was nothing from Neuro but silence.

'The universe is not outside of you. Look inside yourself;
everything that you want, you already are.'

– Rumi

Does happiness elude you?

I climbed the corporate ladder pretty fast. I had the ambition, I had the drive, I was smart, and I was willing to work really hard. This of course fast-tracked me into more responsibilities, more promotions, more money. And every time I hit a new milestone; it was such an adrenaline rush! It was a win for my ego, and everything was about 'what next?'

I was in the rat race—running as fast as I could towards the next piece of cheese. And when I got that cheese, I felt accomplished. I felt satisfied. But soon, the cheese was gone, and I was running again—to the next stop where I might find it. In this whole maze I couldn't see beyond the next piece of cheese. I couldn't see where I was going.

After my chat with Sid, this approach just wasn't working for me. I realized that this social definition of success just left me feeling empty inside. I did not feel truly content. All the achievements, all the material trappings were not truly generating what I thought they should be doing for me. What was I missing?

Whenever I started thinking along these lines, Neuro's voice would pipe up in my head.

'You are overthinking things.'

'There is nothing wrong with your life. Don't make a big deal out of nothing.'

'Focus on work and leave that nonsense dream behind.'

But that dream had had an impact. I couldn't forget it. And so, I decided to bring out my inner Sherlock Holmes. I've always loved detective stories, and it was now time for me to take up an investigation. Except this time, I'd be directing it inwards—deep into my belief system.

My first point of inquiry was to figure out if I am the only one who felt this emptiness? Whom happiness was eluding? So, I spoke to people and found many who felt the same. They were burnt out yet still plodding on. They didn't know how to fix it either! And I am sure if you have picked up this book, you have felt that too.

The ultimate quest in our life should be to be happy and stay happy. The Dalai Lama said that the purpose of our lives is to be happy. Many poets, Sufis, and spiritual seekers have spent their lives in the quest of bliss. Yet, unless we've attained the state of ultimate bliss, or nirvana, that's not how reality feels.

Today, even as material comforts rise, people aren't happy. India ranked 139 out of 149 countries in UN World Happiness Report 2021[1]. We might know happiness conceptually, but we don't have an adequate experience of it. Given the world we live in, we might actually be able to define unhappiness better!

That's not to say we don't feel happiness. We do, but in bursts and in small yet significant moments. It comes like a ray of sunshine once the clouds of stress and anxiety are taken care of.

---

1. https://www.businesstoday.in/current/economy-politics/india-ranks-149th-in-world-happiness-report-2021-finland-tops-the-list/story/434386.html

But why is happiness so fleeting, so transient? Why can't we be happy now and forever? Is that not a possibility? What will it take for us to be happy? What is holding us back from achieving true happiness?

As I dove deeper into these questions, I thought I need to first define what happiness means. Unless you know what you are seeking, you can't expect to find it right? Well, I looked in the most obvious place first. The Oxford Dictionary defines it as 'deep pleasure or contentment in one's circumstances.' That wasn't enough for me, so I kept looking. I did some more research on happiness and found that it isn't all positive emotions or even absence of negative emotions. Rather, emotions are an expression of happiness, not happiness itself. My study pointed me to ancient wisdom that happiness is a paradox or, rather, an empirical irony—the more you chase it, the more it eludes you.

And because pinpointing what happiness means is so difficult, we instead start chasing the generalized beliefs, myths, about happiness—which gets us nowhere! Let's take a look at some of these myths and how they are derailing us from finding happiness in our daily lives.

Myth 1: Happiness and pleasure are synonymous

Have you ever felt excited after a day of shopping?

Felt good after a delicious meal?

Danced a victory jig after trouncing your friend in a game?

These are all pleasurable activities and are good for your mental wellbeing. But this isn't happiness.

Pleasure is momentary, short-lived, and caused by external stimuli. It is simply doing what we enjoy—an indulgence of the senses that triggers dopamine, a neurotransmitter in our brain. Any number of things could be pleasurable—ice cream, food, smoking, alcohol, drugs, sex, buying something and using it… the list goes on. But this high doesn't last. You cannot enjoy your favourite meal on a full stomach. The high from that shopping trip lasts just till you get home. The pleasure from winning a game, lasts only till you get busy with something else. It can even turn to disappointment if you lose the next one! If it's a substance-induced pleasure, once it wears off it can actually lead to dissatisfaction, boredom, lack of satiety, and the desire for a new portion of pleasure.

I have always been goal driven. I've measured my life and success by milestones. Get a job, get promoted, buy a car, buy a house… you get the drift. One of my targets was to buy a luxury SUV before I was 45. Well, I achieved the goal. After we got the SUV, for a few days I was elated. It felt good. The car looked good, was comfortable to drive, and of course it came with an enhanced status. And I enjoyed all of that. There was a bit of a rush when I drove the car, some pride and arrogance also showed up. In fact, it was like a drug high. I thought I would continue to feel this way for a while. But surprise, surprise! Like all highs it didn't last too long. I slogged for years to achieve this but within a few days I no longer felt as good about it as I thought I would. The high had worn off. I had moved on. I got used to the car now and was onto the next chase. It was pleasurable while it lasted, but now I needed something bigger and better to make me feel as good.

The question is, what is the trade-off? Did I go through all that effort, pain, and grind only for a few days of pleasure? Would my next goal also be just fleeting happiness? Am I in for a never-ending chase?

I realized that pleasure is about taking… and the quest for pleasure leads to addiction that could destroy any future happiness. In fact, the more pleasure you seek the unhappier you get! The day you find the awareness that pleasure is just an illusion, 'maya', you will be able to see beyond the mist of this maya.

So, the next time you buy those shoes, or drink that wine, or eat that cake—know what you are experiencing. Don't confuse this pleasure with happiness. **Happiness is a journey, not a destination.** It's the expression of your innermost self. You can give up these pleasures and still be happy. That's what monks do!

Don't worry, I'm not asking you to be a monk. My aim is to make you see the truth—that real happiness is not tied into momentary pleasure.

Then, what is it tied to?

To understand that we must first look at unhappiness. What makes us unhappy?

Bertrand Russell, in his book *The Conquest of Happiness*, explained why people are so unhappy in the modern world. Two of the causes of unhappiness he identified included meaninglessness and boredom[2]. There are several other studies that prove that happiness is tied to the meaning we find in life—our purpose.

The pursuit of happiness then is actually a pursuit of purpose.

Myth 2: Money is the key to happiness

Once upon a time, there was a fisherman who lived in a quiet little coastal village with his family. He had a small boat that he took into the sea early in the morning and returned with a load of fish to sell. He was done selling his fish by 11 in the morning, and he spent the rest of the day relaxing with his friends in the village, spending time with his family, and singing songs in the evening.

One day a rich man came to the village on vacation. He saw the fisherman selling his catch of the day and was impressed by the quality of the fish. He asked the fisherman, 'how much time do you spend fishing?'

'Only a few hours,' said the fisherman. 'I catch enough for our needs.'

'Why don't you spend more time fishing?' asked the rich man.

'What would that do?' the fisherman retorted.

'Well, if you spend more time fishing, you could catch and sell more fish. That would help you buy a bigger boat and hire people to help you catch more fish. Then you can buy more boats, have a staff, move to the city, open a plant to process the fish and sell the final product. You could become rich like me in just a few decades!' said the rich man.

'And what would I do when I am rich?' the fisherman shot back.

'Well, then you can take holidays in little coastal villages, spend time with your friends and family, fish a little, and relax in the evenings.'

Like the rich man in this story, most of us tend to forget that money is not the key to happiness. By that logic, all rich people should be happy.

---

2. https://russell-j.com/beginner/COH-TEXT.HTM

But that's not quite true. Princeton University researchers[3] found that, 'people with above-average income are relatively satisfied with their lives but are barely happier than others in moment-to-moment experience, tend to be more tense, and do not spend more time in particularly enjoyable activities.'

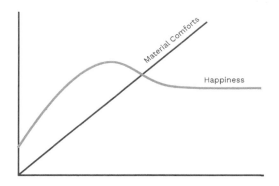

Money can buy you comfort and security, but beyond a point it doesn't have much impact on your happiness. And the trick is also in how you spend your money. People who use money to experience life are generally happier than those who spend money on things.

More money ≠ More happiness

Several studies show that money stops having an impact on your happiness after you reach a certain earning capacity[4]. But we still chase after a bigger paycheck—working insane hours and taking undue stress to get that promotion or pay raise.

What's the use of money if you are so stressed earning it that you die of a heart attack?

But most of us forget that. We chase after these meaningless laurels—heftier bank accounts, new cars, bigger houses—going from one empty success to another; and forget what truly makes us happy. Looking for a better life, we forget to LIVE life itself. We forget that a

---

3. https://www.princeton.edu/news/2006/06/29/link-between-income-and-happiness-mainly-illusion

4. https://www.forbes.com/sites/learnvest/2012/04/24/the-salary-that-will-make-you-happy-hint-its-less-than-75000/?sh=2b3f57d03247

happy and fulfilled life is not of material comforts alone, but of balance in all the important areas of our life.

Myth 3: To be happy I need to control events and circumstances

'We must let go of the life we have planned, so as to accept the one that is waiting for us.'

– Joseph Campbell

It's a well-accepted fact by personal growth pursuers that you cannot control what happens to you. You can only control your response to it.

Life is not a bed of roses for anyone. Buddhism is based on four noble truths, and the first one says, 'Suffering, pain, and misery exist in life.' You will experience pain, fear, grief, loss, scorn, shame. You will have challenges thrown at you every day. Everybody suffers. Both those who have nothing and those who have everything. Those who don't suffer in the present will make the transition to a state of pain at a later date. It might be because of the falling currency or a terrorist attack. It might be when finding out that someone doesn't love him or her anymore. Or they might get upset because they don't get a reply to a message they sent, or if they don't earn enough money, or for any other reason you can think of.

Here's what I want you to think about:

- Suffering exists. We will always find a reason to suffer.

- Life will happen. You cannot control it.

But most of us live life with the illusion that we can control it. All it shows is that you are insecure and uncertain about the future. You cannot know what will happen tomorrow. Not to be morbid, but accidents happen, sickness happens, pandemics happen, black swan events happen. And then when we lose control, we get deeply disturbed. Trying to control everything will not get you anywhere. It's a fear-based need and it doesn't really result in sustained happiness.

'You're the one to talk,' Neuro's voice is strong in my mind. 'Didn't you want your children to behave a certain way? Weren't you looking to gain the favour of your boss? Didn't you feel you'd be happier if your parents could brag about your achievements?'

Guilty as charged! For the longest time, I tried to control every little detail in my life. Look where it got me! In a psychedelic dream with a raven!

But I've realized, no matter how much you try, you are never in control. The game is to focus on acceptance and appreciation of things as they are, without needing to control them.

Myth 4: Happiness is conditional

Let me tell you a story.

Once upon a time a poor man and her son lived in a small town. One day the man decided that he needed to do something about his finances. His idea was to breed horses to make money. But he didn't have the money to buy a stallion and start his business. He really wanted to do this, so he borrowed money from his neighbours and bought a horse.

He, along with his son, built a paddock for the stallion, but the very night the horse came, he broke it and ran away.

The next day people in the town came to gawk at the ruined paddock. They told the man, 'This is so sad. You borrowed money to buy this horse and now you have no horse and no money. How will you pay back your debt? What will happen to your sons' future! Oh! This is so bad!'

The man just shrugged and said, 'Who knows what's good and what's bad.'

A few days later the town was in for a surprise. The stallion that had run away, was found with a group of wild horses. The man was able to entice all these horses to the paddock and this time he took care to ensure they couldn't escape. From one horse he was now the owner of many horses.

The townspeople came again and praised his good fortune. 'You are so lucky. You are so rich now!'

The man again said, 'Who knows what's good and what's bad.'

A few days later while trying to train the horses, the man's son was injured. His leg was broken so badly that it couldn't be fixed properly and left him with a limp.

The neighbours said, 'What a tragedy for such a young man.'

And the man replied, 'Who knows what's good and what's bad.'

The same year, the country found itself at war. The government started recruitment in the army and all able young men were drafted. The draft came to the town and took all the young men except the man's son.

The neighbours wailed, 'our sons have been taken away! What will happen to them!' They told the man, 'You are so lucky to have your son still with you.'

And even then, all the man said was, 'Who knows what's good and what's bad.'

This man had unlocked the secret to happiness. He didn't depend on external occurrences to be happy. He realized that what has happened already can have many consequences and you have no way to determine at that moment whether they are good or bad. He wasn't depending on something happening to make him happy.

He never said, 'when this happens then I will be happy.'

But how many of us have thought that at some point in time?

I will be happy when I get that promotion.

I will be happy when I buy that house.

I will be happy when I can see my children well settled.

I will be happy if the person I like likes me back too.

This is nothing but wishful thinking.

We tend to look at happiness as a destination, and so we justify our dissatisfaction with the current situation. We want to change it. We want to get to the point where we will find happiness. We feel if we get to a milestone, we'll suddenly find happiness.

Not happening, my friend. You know it.

How many times have you heard that happiness is a journey and not the destination? It's high time you start believing it. There is no pot of gold at the end of the rainbow. The beauty is in the rainbow itself.

Evidence[5] suggests that even if you change your life's circumstances, you won't really find the wellbeing you are looking for. Instead, if you make simple changes in your behaviour and mindset now, you are likely to find greater happiness.

Let go of the conditions and enjoy the present moment. Be happy NOW and every day. Don't waste your life waiting for something to happen—you'll only regret it.

Where are you seeking happiness?

Sid told me that I was searching for happiness in the wrong place. He showed me how the key to my happiness was within me. And once I started acting on his advice, my life changed.

Before you go looking for happiness, let me tell you something. Not everyone can be happy. Most of us will be constrained by our own minds, our thinking, our beliefs, and our inability to change.

In practice, consistently happy, calm, balanced, and benevolent people are the ones:

- who have disciplined their minds

- whose minds are trained and capable of not worrying about everything around them

- who manage to retain a sense of joy not only in agreeable circumstances but also in unpleasant situations

Otherwise, there's an endless stream of events, which will evoke only pain, irritation, and anxiety. A person who reacts emotionally to every little incident can never be happy inside.

Happiness means retaining a balance in your mind. It is a state of complete peace of mind, which is achieved by overcoming the blind, automated reactions of the mind to events.

When you dream all day and night of finding your one true love, creating a family, a well-paid job, an opportunity to work for yourself, to travel, you think that you know what happiness is. At least, what

---

5. http://sonjalyubomirsky.com/files/2012/09/Layous-Lyubomirsky-in-press.pdf

your own happiness is. Of course, you can't always be satisfied with everything. And this is fine. The most important thing is that you know what to strive for. Looking at your dreams, you realize where your sense of enduring joy comes from.

If your search for happiness is external, material, and physical in nature, you won't be able to generate that eternal joy within. So, turn around. Look inside. That fountain of happiness is waiting for you!

Remember ships don't sink because of the water around them. They sink when that water gets inside them. Don't let what's happening around you get inside and drown your happiness.

REFLECTION TIME

Scan this QR code to access your Happiness Habits bonus content here:

DISCOVER

Before you go further in this book, take a minute to ask yourself:

Am I chasing the wrong idea of happiness? What are some of the happiness myths I carry?

_____

_____

_____

_____

Take some time to think about the things that give you pleasure versus the things that give you lasting happiness. Make a list.

I find pleasure in...	I find happiness in...
Eating good food	Healthy body
An evening out with friends	Building meaningful relationships
Getting a promotion	Giving back to the needy

Plot your regular day and see how you respond to things that happen. Make a journal and do it over a few weeks. This will give you an idea of how you respond to situations and how you have tethered your happiness.

What happened?	How did I respond to it?	How did it make me feel?	What could I have done instead?

DECIDE

Write down your intent to live a happier life:

_____

_____

_____

_____

_____

_____

STRATEGIZE

Go to your online Happiness Habits experience at *www. happinesshabits.in* and watch the guided visualization on the *'Myths of Happiness'*.

What are some things you can do to let go of your happiness myths and actually find true happiness?

_____

_____

_____

_____

_____

The Pursuit of Happiness

'We're finding that it's not necessarily the reality that shapes us, but the lens through which your brain views the world that shapes your reality. And if we can change the lens, not only can we change your happiness, we can change every single educational and business outcome at the same time.'

– Shawn Achor, author of *The Happiness Advantage*

On a warm summer afternoon, I was thinking about my conversation with Sid. I had been intensively researching happiness since that dream and was trying to make sense of all the information I had gathered. I was analytical by nature and needed to process stuff before acting on it. I was in my study, thinking, when suddenly I found myself on a white sandy beach. The turquoise ocean gleamed like a jewel and the water was so clear that I could see the fish swimming in the shallows. The sun's rays reflecting from the water were shimmering brilliantly. It was an ethereal sight.

I settled down to enjoy the view, noticing that there was no one around. And as I breathed in the salty air, I felt a moment of just pure bliss.

Something or someone, settled down on my right—it was Sid.

'Hi Sid, fancy seeing you here,' I said.

'Well, who else were you expecting?' said the raven. And if ravens could raise eyebrows, I am sure he was doing that.

'So, what brings you here? I thought you were a permanent feature in my head,' I asked.

'Where do you think we are, then?' he retorted.

Ah! Looks like this was another dream and another lesson with this raven who'd decided to be my spirit guide in the quest for happiness.

As if sensing my thoughts, Sid said, 'it's time for your next lesson, my friend.'

'Already? I haven't even processed the previous one, you know,' I exclaimed.

'I know. I've been seeing the gears in your head whirring,' Sid laughed. 'And that's why you need the second lesson. Happiness is not an intellectual concept, it's something that you need to experience. The more you experience it, the sooner it becomes a part of you. Come... I want to show you something.'

In a swirl of colour, we went from the serene beach to a deserted video-game parlour. Sid flew and settled down on a console of a brightly glittering *Game of Happiness*. He tapped it with his beak and looked at me as if saying, 'get on with it.'

I poked around the controls while Sid gave me an overview. 'You have to cross the levels one by one, and every level unlocks more happiness.'

I gave it a try, but I was not able to cross even level one!

Sid watched me fail repeatedly and then gave me a hint with a long-suffering sigh, 'you need to use your secret weapons.'

'Wait, I have weapons?' I retorted.

'Well, this is the quest for happiness, right? How can you go on a quest unarmed?' Sid explained. 'Your weapons are your skills, your intrinsic gifts. As you learn to use them, you'll be able to express yourself better and move faster through the levels.'

'Okay, okay. So, are these weapons the only thing I need?' I asked.

'Well, at least you have learnt to ask some decent questions.' snarked Sid. 'You need to develop some faculties to play the game well. Think of it like driving on a highway. You can drive on reflex—most of us do. We pay less attention to the road and more to what's going on in our head—something someone said, that unpaid loan, or some series on Netflix. But that increases our chances of crashing because we aren't watching the road, we aren't present in the NOW. If you are mindful, focused, and disciplined, you can play this game better. It'll improve your experience.'

'So, use skills to express and be fully present to experience. Got it.' I said as I got back to the game. I unlocked level after level till the video-game parlour became a blur and I blinked awake in my study. Looked like I had a very productive afternoon nap!

The power of choice

My encounter with Sid made me realize that if I want to be happy, I need to take action towards my happiness. I can't sit around and wait for happiness to come to me. Living a good life, a happy life, is a choice we have to make every day.

Unfortunately, most of us just float through life. We don't deliberate on the consequences of the choices we make. We don't realize that in the larger scheme of things, even a small choice can trigger a big difference. A small snowball can become an avalanche. A flap of a butterfly's wings could lead to storms on the other side of the world[6].

6. https://www.forbes.com/sites/startswithabang/2018/02/13/chaos-theory-the-butterfly-effect-and-the-computer-glitch-that-started-it-all/?sh=50b6700a69f6

If the first step on the happiness ladder is to identify what myths we subscribe to, the second step is to take ownership of our happiness. To exercise choice and take responsibility for the consequences of those choices.

Holocaust survivor and psychologist Viktor Frankl famously said, 'everything can be taken from a man but one thing: the last of the human freedoms—to choose one's attitude in any given set of circumstances, to choose one's own way.'

Choice is the most powerful of weapons in your arsenal. You can CHOOSE your life and how it shapes up. If Viktor Frankel[7] could practise choosing his response in the midst of the horrors of concentration camps, I am sure we can do it in our mundane lives.

And with every choice you make, you are either moving forward into growth or stepping back to perceived safety where there is no growth and, possibly, no happiness.

I had a friend who was, by admission, super lazy. He would crib about lethargy, and having no energy, being irritable and feeling sluggish all the time, but he would sit on his couch all day and watch TV or play games or take calls. On the off-days when he exercised—went for a walk or did a few stretches—he admitted that it made him feel better. He felt more energized, more focused, and was in a better mood. It was clear to everyone (even him!) that a few minutes of exercise daily meant a better, happier, more productive day for him—yet he did not make that choice. Playing a video game was giving him that momentary pleasure while exercising was a pain. And so, he wasn't motivated enough to take the pain!

We are going to talk a lot more about motivation in the coming pages. But for now, I just wanted to highlight that even these small things can have a massive, cumulative effect on your overall happiness and wellbeing.

We all do this. We choose momentary pleasures over pain or discomfort. It's the *law of least effort* at play—we all want to choose the easiest way to do something. And not just physically, we make these choices emotionally too.

It's easy to blame someone else for our lot in life.

---

7. https://www.brainpickings.org/2013/03/26/viktor-frankl-mans-search-for-meaning/

It's easy to push the onus of your feelings on someone else.

It's easy to say, 'I had no choice, it happened to me.'

It's easy to think, 'but what could I have done?'

Well, what's easy is not always good for you. Your happiness or unhappiness is no one's responsibility but yours. So, take a stand! Take ownership! And go out there and do what makes you happy!

I've been faced with this pleasure or pain, safety or growth dilemma often enough. I was in a well-paid and comfortable job. I had a good set of friends, and my boss was very nice to me. My team was good, and I had been there in the role for a while and made a difference. People knew me, appreciated me, and I was settled. At this point, the promoters of this firm decided to set up a startup firm and I had an option of moving there. But I would have to leave behind my boss, my friends, a large part of my team, and in the new setup my role would be smaller, and it was not a known firm, so it would have lesser brand value. Logically, it did not make much sense to move and that was what most of my peers chose.

Why leave a comfortable, stable, well-paying, and cushy job?

My heart, though, wanted the startup option. 'Think about the learning, the growth, the challenge. Think about what you could build and the difference you'd make,' it whispered to me.

If I hadn't started on my quest for happiness, I'd perhaps do what my peers had done and stayed back in safety. But I knew happiness is in following your heart—so I took that leap of faith and joined the startup. People thought I was crazy to do that; what they didn't know was that this move made me come alive!

The path to happiness is through expression and experiences.

The pursuit of happiness requires us to be in touch with our inner calling, understand what matters more to us, and then make those tough choices that are in alignment with who we are.

Abraham Maslow said, 'what one can be, one must be!' We are wired to become what we are destined to be. There is an inner urge that pushes you towards your potential. If you ignore that, unhappiness raises its ugly head. Moving from where you are towards where the purpose of your soul is, moves you towards happiness.

True happiness lies in being able to express ourselves fully and experience life completely in all its glory.

Expression comes from doing what we love—that's when you unleash your potential and seize the day. That's when you are at your most efficient and effective. Expression is also about bringing forth your unique gifts and contributing to a greater good beyond ourselves.

Experience is about being fully present in every moment of life—understanding that the present moment is all you have. Experiencing life is also about learning from it to grow into better versions of ourselves.

Living a good life requires that we bring our best version to the fore every day. Think of it like being a triathlete. Staying on top of the game requires being in top form across multiple dimensions. If you stop practising, you lose your edge. And most urban professionals forget an important aspect of this game—to be able to bring your best version to EVERY aspect of life.

RAVEN : IT'S ALL IN THE HEAD

Most of us are not able to express or experience the best version of ourselves because we don't even know what that is. We are so attuned to what someone else has decided for us, that we never really give it much thought. We also live in fear, chasing the wrong idea of happiness, and enveloped in negative mindsets. There is so much drama in life, who has the time to think about these things, right? WRONG! By not choosing to discover your true self, you are doing yourself a disservice.

And I was guilty of it too.

I was constantly working, missing out on important family responsibilities because of project deadlines, and feeling exhausted and burnt out. Sounds familiar? I was choosing to perform in one dimension of life and neglecting the rest.

'But what choice did you have? You had to work to earn a good living, get promoted, and be successful,' pipes up Neuro, my ever-present reality-check.

Sid's faint voice echoes in my mind, 'you were making a choice. But those choices were not in your best interest. They were piling up and making you unhappy. And that's why you had to break free of this destructive construct.'

You too need to figure out the mental construct you are operating from and see if it is serving you. If it's not, then it's time to break free! Evolve your mindset to one that supports happiness and practise the things that will move you forward.

Your happiness will come from:

- Realizing that happiness is a choice

- Choosing to accept your circumstances and relinquishing the need for control

- Understanding and pursuing your purpose

- Being *independent*—i.e., depending on your inner self and not external factors

- Your motivation, values, and mindset

- Being present in the moment and enjoying it to the fullest

- Learning and growing to be a better person

Let me tell you right here that it's not going to be easy. The biggest obstacle to your quest for happiness will be your own ego. Your ego blocks new knowledge; it pipes up and says, 'this is useless,' or 'I know this already.' And once you say this, you block any ability to absorb anything new because you've concluded that you are already aware of it. Your ego doesn't allow you to open up to new thinking or new experiences blocking your way to happiness.

Even if you do surpass your ego, finding true happiness will require you to CONSCIOUSLY generate positive feelings and emotions by changing your beliefs, thoughts, actions, and feelings. It will require you to CONSCIOUSLY practise *Happiness Habits*. And it will require you to CONSCIOUSLY bring balance to all aspects of your life—Health, Relationships, Abundance, Spirituality, Parenting, Career, Social, etc.

To do this, you need to get into a happiness mindset. You need to dive deeper within yourself—become more self-aware, manage yourself better, and release the blocks that are holding you back. Let's talk about that in the next chapter. For now, some reflection time!

REFLECTION TIME

DISCOVER

What makes me happy and what does happiness look like to me?

_____

_____

_____

_____

_____

What results would be needed to make me feel happy?

_____

_____

_____

_____

How can I own my happiness?

_____

_____

_____

_____

What choices have I made recently that have made me unhappy? Why did I make those choices?

_____

_____

_____

_____

_____

_____

DECIDE

What are the choices that I need to make today to experience happiness?

_____

_____

_____

_____

_____

_____

_____

_____

_____

STRATEGIZE

How will I implement these choices into my life?

_____

_____

_____

_____

_____

_____

_____

_____

Happiness Mindset

'Your beliefs become your thoughts,

Your thoughts become your words,

Your words become your actions,

Your actions become your habits,

Your habits become your values,

Your values become your destiny.'

– Mahatma Gandhi

Have you ever thought about who you are?

What makes you, 'you'?

How are you different from the billions of other people in the world?

Why are even identical twins different people?

'You' are your thoughts, your beliefs, your values, your feelings—an amalgamation of experiences and actions. You've been forged through childhood conditioning, social constructs, familial bonds, expectations, etc. You are a product of your environment, shaped by your life situations. You are the stories you tell yourself.

If you change your story… you can change your life!

Your day-to-day system operates on this programming you have built over time—your mindset. Your mindset, essentially, is the set of beliefs you carry that shape your worldview—both internal (how you see yourself) and external. It influences how you think, feel, and behave in any given situation. And the more you lean towards a particular belief or feeling, the harder your coding becomes in that area.

Swami Mukundananda, in his book *7 Mindsets for Success, Happiness and Fulfilment*, said, 'Thoughts and feelings that persist over time harden into an attitude. If you live with an attitude long enough it becomes second nature—a mindset. The wrong mindset could lead you off the path of contentment, joy, enlightenment. The right one will point you to the road to success, to fulfilment and towards and towards an extraordinary life.'

Our brain is essentially a pattern-recognition engine. So, when you repeatedly do similar things, it starts recognizing a pattern and remembers it. The next time, it's likely to pick out that information over all else—like a social media algorithm or a search engine. When you search for a specific term or look at a certain type of content over the Internet—you are more likely to be shown a similar type of content. For instance, what shows up first in your social feed is determined by what posts and accounts you engage with the most. That limits your worldview. A similar thing happens with your mind too.

'The mind has a powerful way of attracting things that are in harmony with it, good and bad.'

– Idowu Koyenikan

When you think or behave a certain way, you are more likely to find resonating thoughts or actions in your environment. That's because your mind is isolating everything else and just showing you what you've already programmed in.

Haemin Sunim, in his book *The Things You Can See Only When You Slow Down*, summarizes this beautifully. He says, 'When we look at the outside world, we are looking at only a small part that interests us. The world we see is not the entire universe but a limited one that the mind cares about. However, to our minds, that small world is the entire universe. Our reality is not the infinitely stretching cosmos but the small part we choose to focus on.'

Does that mean you are creating unhappiness for yourself by choosing to look for negative things? Totally! But the good thing is, once you know this, you can fix it. Let's figure out how you are doing it in the first place.

We've got millions of years of information coded into our genes that is called our survival instinct. This is the information that helped our ancestors survive the wild and kept them alive. Unfortunately, the survival instinct is coded for fear. It keeps you alert about things to watch out for, things that can harm you. It doesn't bother about things that keep you happy—after all, happiness isn't essential for *survival*. So, picking up on the negative is the natural inclination of our minds. And you'll see it everywhere.

Just try and observe a casual conversation anywhere. After the usual pleasantries it quickly devolves into the negative. Things that aren't working. Stuff that is going wrong. People who are no good at what they do. Bosses who are tyrannical. Jobs that are unfulfilling. It's an endless stream of complaints! And the thing is, more often than not we don't even know it. It's become second nature to us! And the whole environment supports this tendency. Take the news—it only highlights the negative, the headlines screaming what's wrong with the world and sensationalizing it even more to get our fear attuned senses to take note. Take social media—just crawling with trolls everywhere!

And this tendency has aggravated in recent years. Once you have put up a post on social media, it feels like a job done. You've pointed out that children are starving, forests are burning, or that the national identity is in crisis. And so have a million other people. You've given away the onus of action—so easy!

But I digress.

What I wanted to say was that we are naturally inclined to the negative. And today when we are bombarded with information—we get as much information daily as someone living 200 years ago would have got in their lifetime, and the magnitude of negativity has amplified. We have normalized negativity! Everyone is complaining, so it's okay! Your negative mindset gets reinforced with every new interaction, and you start believing in it more strongly. So begins your descent into an unhappiness spiral. And when we reinforce it over and over, it becomes our mindset. And living with a negative mindset is like a magnet for unhappiness!

Most of us have become programmed for unhappiness. This is the reason why happiness is still scarce despite us being in the most comfortable place in the entire history of humankind.

'If you think adventure is dangerous, try routine, it is lethal.'

– Paulo Coelho

THE UNHAPPY SPIRAL

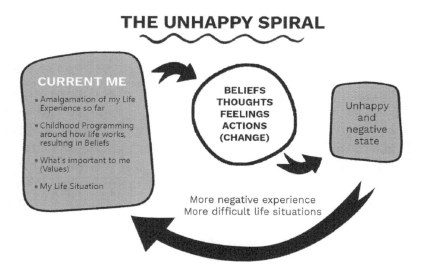

CURRENT ME
- Amalgamation of my Life Experience so far
- Childhood Programming around how life works, resulting in Beliefs
- What's important to me (Values)
- My Life Situation

BELIEFS
THOUGHTS
FEELINGS
ACTIONS
(CHANGE)

Unhappy and negative state

More negative experience
More difficult life situations

For the longest time, I was operating from a place of fear. Whatever happened in my life, I first looked at it from a lens of what could go wrong. I would immediately start thinking about the worst-case scenario and start getting stressed and anxious about it. I thought I was being cautious, but instead I was sabotaging my own happiness and peace of mind!

'Hey! You were not all that different. Isn't everyone around you doing the same thing?' Neuro chimed in. 'And really, you can't change who you are.'

'Oh! So, if I believe I'm worthless there is no way of changing that?' snarked Sid.

'Hey! No one is calling anyone worthless,' grumbled Neuro. 'But if you've lived all your life a certain way, you can't just change.'

'Let's wait and watch, shall we?' I could hear the smile in Sid's voice.

They leave me with an interesting question—***can we re-programme ourselves?***

And when I found the answer, it was a resounding YES! I've tried it, and it works!

So how do we do that? How do you break out of this unhappiness spiral? How do you shatter patterns that don't serve you?

Let me introduce you to a neuro-linguistic programming (NLP) technique called **Pattern Interrupt**. This tried and tested technique could be your ticket to creating Happiness Habits. Pattern Interrupt does exactly what its name suggests. It interrupts your existing pattern and makes space for a new one.

Stage 1: Awareness

The first step towards change is the awareness that something needs change. You need to think through what makes you happy. How is your actual happiness different from the happiness myths you are subscribing to? What are the things you can do that will help you bring forward your best expression? What can you shift to be able to experience life in every moment for all that it has to offer?

When you are aware of who you are, where you are, what you need to do, and WHY, it becomes easier to move forward.

Stage 2: Action

When you are ready to move forward, you need to work on changing the limiting beliefs that might be holding you back. This change comes from a *pattern interrupt* action. When you recognize that you are falling into your old pattern, you take action that stops that downward spiral. Over and above that, inculcate practices in your day that enforce more positive and happy thinking.

For instance, the practice of gratitude. If you spend 5 minutes at the beginning and end of each day being grateful for what you have, you'll automatically see a more positive outlook building in life. And as you drive that wedge of gratitude deeper into your negative mindset, you'll open up to possibilities. Change starts to happen as you take action and you create a new, stronger, more positive pathway in your brain that overrides the limiting belief. So now when a neuron transmits a signal and hits the decision point, 'what do I do in this situation,' it takes the more positive route instead of the usual one that would have led to negativity.

Stage 3: Habit formation and belief restructuring

When you stop reinforcing a limiting belief, you make space to create a new, empowering one. A change in your beliefs leads to a change in thoughts, feelings, and emotions. And that leads to more positive actions and positive outcomes. As you keep practising your new beliefs and reinforcing them with new actions, you'll discover what is really important to you. And you'll find that you are living the life that you always wanted—one full of happiness and contentment.

Once you move through these three steps, it improves your overall experience and life situation, shifting you to a permanent happiness mindset.

Let's see how this works with an example. We all know that staying active is a key ingredient for happiness as it keeps us in good health. One of the ways to stay active is to be regular with your fitness regime. But most of us find that difficult right? I know I did!

'I'm tired, I'll go to the gym tomorrow.'

'Gym can wait, I have an urgent call to take.'

'It's fine if I miss one day.'

Sounds familiar?

This is a pattern that's not serving you. This is a pattern that's probably making you more tired and sluggish. This is a pattern that needs breaking. And it might be coming from an underlying belief such as 'I am lazy' or 'I don't care about fitness'.

To break that, we need to find some simple actions and tie them with a handy trigger.

Let's say you decide to walk to the washroom and splash water on your face every time you think of missing the gym. And immediately after you tie your shoelaces and pick up your gym bag.

OR

You decide to do five jumping jacks every time you think of missing the gym. And immediately after you tie your shoelaces and pick up your gym bag.

These are now your triggers and actions. Every time you splash water on your face or do jumping jacks, it's a trigger to tie your shoelaces and pick up your gym bag. You are mentally ready to go to the gym!

As you repeat these triggers and actions over and over again, for every block and limiting belief you hold, you'll find yourself stepping into a positive and growth mindset—the mindset primed for happiness and fulfilment.

Mindset Matters!

Many years ago, I was working in Mangalore as the Location HR Head for a large IT firm. We had many housekeeping staff who helped maintain the place. Among these folks was a young boy called Vaman Pai. He came from an economically backward family and had been supporting them from a young age. Due to this, he had limited education and not many job opportunities.

But this kid didn't let life bring him down!

In most companies, the housekeeping staff is invisible. They do what's assigned to them and only interact with their supervisor at best. Vaman, on the other hand, was everywhere. He offered his help to everyone and wanted to do more than what his job required. He was always smiling, always willing. And that attitude got him noticed.

We felt that he had potential and decided to invest in him. We moved him from housekeeping to an office boy and started him off on computers. We encouraged him to learn to write and speak in English, and he worked on that. Gradually, he started doing well and picked up things that were done by regular employees and soon he was absorbed as an employee. In the history of that company, such a thing had never happened before— there was a lot of emphasis on the quality of hires and for this young kid to make the cut was a really big deal.

Once in a while, Vaman calls me to wish me on my birthday and his story often reminds me what a big difference a positive mindset can make.

In contrast to Vaman's story are the countless fresh graduates who join a company and feel entitled to certain privileges because of their pedigree. They don't want to learn the ropes, but can be found around water coolers discussing how everything sucks, how the manager doesn't know what he/she is doing, how the culture is bad, and so on. Invariably these folks go through a downward spiral and end up leaving a company.

How you think about a situation makes a massive difference to your happiness. Take the Olympics, for example. Several studies[8] prove that bronze medallists are generally happier than silver medallists. That's counterintuitive right? But it's true. And it's all in the thought process. This happens because of a phenomenon called counterfactual thinking.

There is a human tendency to create possible alternatives to life events that have already happened, which would be contrary to what actually happened. In this case, the silver medallist thinks, "Oh, I couldn't win the gold," while the bronze medallist thinks, "At least, I got a medal." So, in the athlete's mind, the silver medal is won after losing, but a bronze medal is won after winning.

When you apply this thought process to life, you often end up not appreciating what you have. You aren't grateful for the silver, but lament the gold. And that is the cause for unhappiness.

---

8. https://www.npr.org/2021/07/29/1022537817/theres-a-psychology-lesson-behind-why-olympic-bronze-medalists-are-so-happy

Mindsets for a happier life

In your quest for happiness and fulfilment, two mindsets will serve you:

- A positive mindset, and

- A growth mindset

Think Positive

A negative mindset focuses on the negative side of people, experiences, situations, or judgments. The example I gave earlier about casual conversations was a negative mindset on display. A positive mindset, on the other hand, focuses on the bright side of life. It attunes you to make the most of any situation and approach life's challenges expecting positive outcomes. A positive mindset helps you see yourself, your abilities, and other people in a positive light. A positive mindset is built on the pillars of optimism, resilience, acceptance, gratitude, integrity, and mindfulness[9].

Negative Mindset	Positive Mindset
Being upset at someone's success	Complimenting someone's success
Getting affected by someone else's negativity	Not letting someone's negativity bring you down
Thinking that nothing good will come of a tough situation	Believing that something good will come from the tough situation you are facing
Being dissatisfied with what you have got	Finding joy in little things

Don't stagnate

In the journey to happiness, it's important to keep moving. Happiness is about putting your best self forward, and that cannot happen if you are stuck in one place. People with fixed mindsets fear change—they are insecure—and so they become distrustful, defensive, and struggle to recover from setbacks that are part and parcel of life. The key to happiness lies in cultivating a growth mindset—a grasp on reality, an inclination for improvement, and a deep desire to take action.

---

9. https://positivepsychology.com/positive-mindset/

A good example is the recent COVID-19 crisis. People with fixed mindsets blame the authorities, the system, the media, the industry—everyone except themselves. They despair of what's happening in the world, and they sit and crib about it. They only see what's going wrong and how it's affecting them—giving little thought to what they can do about it. While people with a growth mindset are out there creating support groups, rallying resources, volunteering—they are taking action! They are the ones who will go home with the satisfaction of having done something and the warmth of people's gratitude and good wishes.

Fixed Mindset	Growth Mindset
I can't do anything about that	If I try hard enough, I might see a way to solve this
Why fix what's not broken?	How can I improve on this?
The government is doing nothing about climate change	If I help plant more trees, I can make a small contribution to fighting climate change

As an urban working professional, your happiness and growth depend on your ability to cultivate these mindsets. Life will never be without its challenges, but these mindsets will be your power—your armour against unhappiness, dissatisfaction, and apathy.

So, how do you go about developing these mindsets? We'll talk about that in the next section where we take on seven happiness quests.

10 Happiness Mindset Statements

1. I put my complete focus and attention on the present.

2. I am stimulated with my work and enjoy what I am doing.

3. I take complete ownership and persist till I achieve the desired outcome.

4. I focus on finding solutions rather than getting discouraged by problems.

5. I look for opportunities to learn and grow.

6. I am aware of the emotional triggers (setbacks and criticism) and take the time out to deal with them.

7. I work towards building trust in my relationships.

8. I am aware of my strengths, capabilities, and talents and am able to leverage them to my advantage.

9. I stand up for what is right.

10. I trust that I am on the right path.

REFLECTION TIME

DISCOVER

Take the *'Is Your Thinking Pattern Cut Out for Happiness?'* quiz in the Happiness Habits bundle.

What is my level of self-awareness about myself—my personality, my thinking, etc.?

_____

_____

_____

_____

Identify some negative thoughts and beliefs I carry.

_____

_____

_____

_____

_____

Identify some fixed thoughts and beliefs I carry.

_____

_____

_____

_____

_____

_____

DECIDE

What can I do to change the negative beliefs I identified and create a positive mindset?

_____

_____

_____

_____

_____

_____

What can I do to change my fixed beliefs and create a growth mindset?

_____

_____

_____

_____

_____

_____

STRATEGIZE

Head over to the Happiness Habits bundle online and listen to the *'Guided Meditation for a Happier Mindset'.*

Start a gratitude journal and use it to celebrate the small, positive moments daily.

What are some positive words and statements about myself and my life? Use them more often in conversations.

_____

_____

_____

_____

_____

_____

_____

What can I do to generate more positivity and growth in my life?

_____

_____

_____

_____

_____

How to Live a Life Full of Happiness

"'I can't see a way through," said the boy.

"Can you see your next step?"

"Yes."

"Just take that," said the horse.'

– Charlie Mackesy

The Seven Quests for Happiness

'Motivation is what gets you started.
Habit is what keeps you going.'

– Jim Rohn

A note on the science of wellbeing

Happiness and wellbeing are two sides of the same coin. While happiness means different things to different people, it is inevitably linked to their wellbeing. People with higher levels of wellbeing[10]:

- Perform better at work
- Have more satisfying relationships
- Are more cooperative
- Have stronger immune systems
- Have better physical health
- Live longer
- Have fewer sleep problems
- Have lower levels of burnout
- Have greater self-control

Dr Martin Seligman, in his book Flourish, defined five building blocks of wellbeing—called the PERMA™ theory of wellbeing. These include:

1. **Positive Emotion:** This entails increasing positive emotions about the past, present, or future. Gratitude, forgiveness,

---

10. https://ppc.sas.upenn.edu/learn-more/perma-theory-well-being-and-perma-workshops

mindfulness, hope, and optimism play a big role in this aspect. However, there is a limit to how much positive emotion a person can feel. Therefore, relying on just this one element for our happiness is not the best course of action.

2. **Engagement:** When you put all your energies, skills, and strengths towards tackling a challenge you experience engagement or a state of flow. This experience is gratifying, and the activity is its own reward. You are fully absorbed in the moment, and it feels as if 'time stopped.' You can find engagement in many things—an engaging conversation, a hobby, or even play.

3. **Relationships:** Humans are social beings and as such relationships amplify our sense of wellbeing. A connection with others gives us more meaning and more acceptance. We laugh more together, we share our sorrows to let go of them, we find love, compassion, kindness, empathy in these social constructs.

4. **Meaning:** This is the crux of our existence. What are we here for? What are we serving? What is our purpose? We find meaning in many things—it could be a social cause, it could be family, religion, or even politics!

5. **Accomplishment:** A sense of accomplishment also adds to our wellbeing. It's about achievement for its own sake. We want to excel at work, in sport, in creative pursuits because it makes us feel competent and successful.

Our wellbeing, to a varying degree, depends on these five elements.

Happiness Unlocked

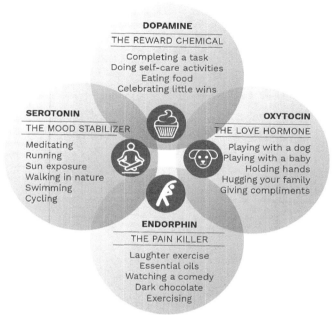

**HAPPINESS CHEMICALS
AND HOW TO HACK THEM**

DOPAMINE

THE REWARD CHEMICAL

Completing a task
Doing self-care activities
Eating food
Celebrating little wins

SEROTONIN

THE MOOD STABILIZER

Meditating
Running
Sun exposure
Walking in nature
Swimming
Cycling

OXYTOCIN

THE LOVE HORMONE

Playing with a dog
Playing with a baby
Holding hands
Hugging your family
Giving compliments

ENDORPHIN

THE PAIN KILLER

Laughter exercise
Essential oils
Watching a comedy
Dark chocolate
Exercising

There is a science behind happiness, and small, simple changes go a long way in building a happier life.

Living your best life—one that is happy and fulfilled, and that brings forth your peak performance—is a five-dimensional construct. It involves understanding, practising, expressing and experiencing, feeling, and being.

1. **Understanding** yourself and your purpose

2. **Practising** gratitude, spirituality, compassion, love, peace, acceptance, tolerance, mindfulness, and forgiveness

3. **Expressing** your talents and your true uninhibited self and being present to experience life in every moment

4. **Feeling** contentment and joy and a connection to your family, your purpose, and finding meaning in life

5. **Being** abundant in all aspects of life that matter to you such as health, wealth, relationships, parenting, and career.

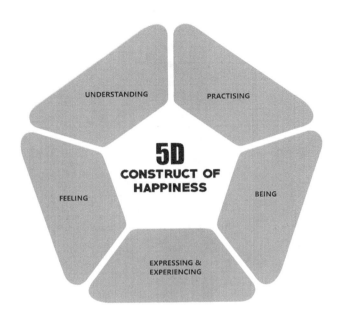

True bliss lies at the pinnacle of this construct. For a monk or a yogi, it's relatively easy to find this bliss. They are not distracted by the mundane, day-to-day realities of life. They can practise silence and meditation whenever they want. There is no boss asking for daily progress reports, children wanting help on their homework, spouses wanting some attention, bills needing to be paid, or cooks taking off. No, that is our lot in life—a life we have chosen.

'Should we leave everything and take the monk's road to bliss then?' came Neuro's agitated voice. 'What is even the point of that! Why do you have to change everything in your life for some random happiness?'

'No one is asking you to be a monk!' Sid shot back. 'The whole point is in finding happiness in your life as it is right now! Something that's practical. Which is why what I am going to tell you is something that anyone can do.'

'Go on then, let's see what you've got,' grumbled Neuro.

And so, Sid explained to me the concept of the seven quests.

To unlock a new level of happiness, you need to achieve a certain level of mastery in each of the seven quests. The level of mastery gets tougher at every level. And when you have 100% mastered all quests, you attain bliss.

MINDFULNESS

HEALING

BETTER ME

LIVING IN THE FLOW

PURSUIT OF PURPOSE

EMOTIONAL MASTERY

BALANCE IN LIFE

These aren't difficult quests. You won't be meditating for hours or depriving any of your senses. These quests are designed to fit the life of an urban professional. Mastery comes from small, actionable changes that anyone can make in their daily life. That, perhaps, is the most important aspect of these quests—daily practise.

We talked about how happiness is linked to mindset. Orienting to a more positive and growth mindset is a long-term game. You can't change it overnight. Just like how top athletes and best musicians practise every day, to be the best version of yourself you need practise to make progress. To ensure that progress is not skewed in any one area of life, equal emphasis needs to be placed on each of the seven quests. These quests are interconnected—if you aren't balanced in all these areas, something or the other will pull you down.

For example, if you are on the quest to become a 'Better Me,' you can't move ahead on it unless you have some level of emotional mastery, some healing, and some balance in life, as well. If you lose focus on those quests, you may find yourself stuck on the quest to become a better version of yourself. For instance, if your relationships aren't going well, or your health is suffering, you will be stressed and will not be able to focus on living a virtuous life.

These quests aren't steps to be taken one after the other, rather they are like moving forward in expanding circles. The progress you make on one quest feeds into another, and to move beyond a certain point in any quest, you have to make equivalent progress in others—else you'll find yourself getting stuck.

In the coming chapters we'll go over each of these quests to understand what they are and how you can take easy, actionable steps to master them.

REFLECTION TIME

DISCOVER

Take a moment to rate yourself on a scale of 1–10 on each of these parameters.

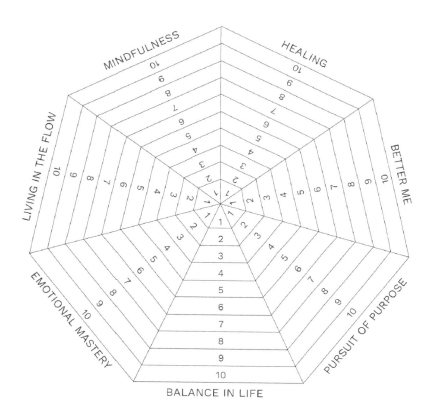

DECIDE

In the above chart, mark on a scale of 1 to 10 where you would want to be in each of these areas at the end of this year.

STRATEGIZE

Download the above chart, '*Rate Yourself on the Seven Quests*', from your online Happiness Habits Bundle and pin it somewhere you can see it daily.

Think about a few things that could help you move forward in each of these areas.

_____

_____

_____

_____

_____

_____

Better Me

'When you do things from your soul, you find a river of joy within you.'

– Rumi

Let me give you a heads-up right here. This is going to be a heavy chapter. We'll talk about stuff that might feel like it's going over your head—but trust me, it's super important if you want to find lasting happiness.

There are two important things we'll talk about in this chapter.

Am I in sync with who I am?

Am I doing what I was put here to do? Am I aspiring to be better?

Being in alignment with who you are

The first step to being happy and in harmony is to be who you are. To be in alignment with what is important to you and reflect that in your life—decisions, actions, and behaviour. If you aren't true to yourself, you are living a life of dissatisfaction and discontent. Most of us end up living a life we think we want, but don't resonate with. Often our worldview is shaped by social expectations, peer pressure, and ego more than our heart's desire. And that might give us a social standing, but never true happiness.

But how do you find out what's important to you? How do you look beyond the noise that's constantly being thrown at you, and discover what you truly cherish?

There are several researchers who've worked to define what we value as humans. They've analysed multiple religions, philosophies, and cultures and defined models of human virtues. One of the most popular models is that of Martin Seligman[11] that defines six most important virtues for humankind, supported by 24-character strengths.

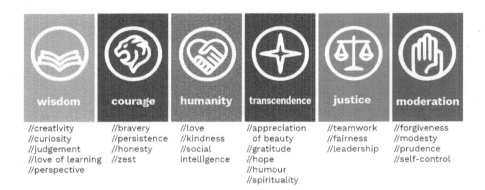

wisdom	courage	humanity	transcendence	justice	moderation
//creativity	//bravery	//love	//appreciation of beauty	//teamwork	//forgiveness
//curiosity	//persistence	//kindness	//gratitude	//fairness	//modesty
//judgement	//honesty	//social intelligence	//hope	//leadership	//prudence
//love of learning	//zest		//humour		//self-control
//perspective			//spirituality		

Similarly, there is Brian Johnson's *Optimize Virtue Compass*[12] that outlines the virtues of wisdom, gratitude, love, curiosity, hope, self-mastery, zest, and courage.

There is usually a misalignment of who we are *versus* what we do. For example, if your aspiration is to live with integrity, ask yourself if you live by this virtue. 'Do I demonstrate integrity when no one is watching? Do I demonstrate integrity in difficult circumstances and under pressure? What if my company asks me to bribe someone to win a deal, would I do it?'

It's important to put a plan around bridging this gap. There are three steps to becoming a better version of yourself:

Discover what's important: There are several virtues, by definition, and you need to identify which ones are important to you. Referring to some of the models I mentioned will give you an idea of the virtues and character traits that appeal to you. You need to get a sense of what feels like 'you' whether you are able to act on it or not. You can take the *VIA Survey of Character Strengths*[13] to take stock of the virtues and character strengths you live by.

---

11. https://positivepsychology.com/classification-character-strengths-virtues/

12. https://optimizehq.s3.amazonaws.com/coach/downloads/worksheets/coach-ii-iv-iii-optimize-virtue-compass.pdf

13. https://www.authentichappiness.sas.upenn.edu/questionnaires/survey-character-strengths

Figure out what's missing: Once you know what's important to you, assess how you embody these virtues in your everyday life. When you are figuring out where you stand, it's important to tell the truth to yourself. More often than not, we want to believe something so badly that we lie to ourselves. We create a belief based on that lie. And that belief doesn't serve us in the quest for happiness because it's based on something that doesn't exist. So, if you believe yourself to be forgiving, take a conscious look at your actions and see how often you demonstrate forgiveness. Only when you are truthful, you can know where you stand and what you need to do for happiness.

Have a plan to arrive from point A to point B: Take consistent action to bring in a change to your beliefs and values and live these virtues every day. Remember that what you value and who you are will change over time, so check-in with yourself consistently to stay on the right course.

In this process, when you are able to turn these virtues into habits and practise them every day, you build character. Your character is the sum of your personality traits. It is who you are on the inside. Your character determines how you live on the outside. A good character is an embodiment of your prized virtues, and it affects everything in your life—it shapes your life. It helps you develop the personality traits you need to manifest the life you want. It helps you become the person you need to be to live the life you want. So, the next time you are faced with a choice to demonstrate integrity, compassion, forgiveness, or any other virtue, you do the right thing—and the urge to do the right thing comes from within.

For example, if the virtue you prize is moderation, and your character trait is forgiveness, you'll be able to put the past behind you. You will be able to forgive the transgressions others have made towards you and move forward in life. You won't be stuck with feelings of hurt or vengeance. By practising forgiveness, you would be able to let go of the negative emotions and focus on the positive. And this change will be intrinsic so that when faced with a situation where you are wronged, you won't have a vengeful thought. Your whole mindset makes a positive shift, and this is how you would be able to find more happiness in your life.

Once you've found alignment with who you are, it's time to think bigger and to aspire for a better version of yourself—something that is much more eternal and cosmically directed.

Fulfilling your soul's purpose

'Nothing ever goes away until it has taught us what we need to know.'

– Pema Chödrön

In one of my visits with Sid, I found myself floating around like a bubble—a very tiny one at that, almost like a droplet of water. There are millions of bubbles around me, and somehow, we all seem connected. I'm enjoying the floating sensation, before I am rudely interrupted by the raven.

'Pay attention! Do you feel anything?' he asked.

Now that he mentioned it, I felt a vibration in the air. It seemed to be saying something to us bubbles, 'you are all just like me, you are a part of me in fact, you are me.'

'But who are you?' I blurted out.

'That's the Big Energy (BE), the source of all creation,' said Sid.

Somehow, floating there as a bubble, I found it hard to dispute that fact. 'But how can a tiny bubble like me be the source of all creation? Didn't BE say I was it?' I wondered.

'All in good time,' replied Sid. 'First let me explain to you who you are.'

And so began my introduction to my soul's purpose. Let me give you some insights from this lesson.

Did you know your soul has a purpose? Ok, hear me out before you dismiss this.

We are mortal beings, right? And when we die, we cannot take anything with us. Even our bodies integrate and go back into nature. The only thing that is not destroyed is the energy we are made of— some call it the soul. Remember the First Law of Thermodynamics? It states that energy is always conserved; it cannot be created or destroyed. So, the soul carries on. But where does it go?

In my studies I have come to believe that there are two paths open to a soul—one takes it to *Nirvana* or the ultimate bliss, and the other brings it back to Earth to learn what it still needs to learn. As a soul in transit, you were put on this Earth to do more than just earn money or seek pleasure. You are here to do things that you were meant to do and learn lessons that will peel away layers of ignorance from your soul. The soul will be reincarnated as long as it still needs to learn something. And in life, you will be presented with situations that help you learn that lesson—you have the free will to either learn it or not.

Let's say, for example, your soul needs to learn forgiveness. Now in life you'll be presented with circumstances where you'll need to learn how to forgive people. You can be stubborn and hold the grudge, but you'll keep getting into those situations till you learn what you were meant to. Or, if you need to learn compassion, you will be presented with situations that require compassion. If you don't work on these lessons, the pain in your life will increase—that's the way of the universe to force your attention on issues that need to be fixed.

The catch is that when you begin your life, you don't know what lessons you are meant to learn.

When we understand this, it's easy to understand that, as human beings, our *dharma* is to constantly become a better version of ourselves. But that purpose often gets lost in the everyday. This book is my attempt at reconnecting you with the inner divine, because that's at the core of everything we will talk about. The quest for happiness is centred on the quest to become a better version of yourself—to Be Good and Do Good.

What is this better version? How do I know what lessons I am supposed to learn? And how long will it take? Well, as long as you need!

Almost every religion says that we have God within us. If you look at mythology and read about Gods that walked the Earth, you'll notice some traits they have in their human *avatars*. These traits—forgiveness, compassion, love, acceptance, truth, etc., are manifestations of your inner divinity. But for us, these traits are covered with layers of ignorance. We've blocked our light from shining. To become better humans, we need to aspire for divinity and live a virtuous life. What would Gods be like as humans? What virtues would they have? Where am I in comparison and what do I need to learn?

To be a good human, you need to consciously and honestly work on your virtues and character traits. When you do that, you will most likely encounter your soul's mission or 'learning need' in this life. And the faster you bridge the gap, the quicker your ascension to bliss.

Of course, you may choose not to care about this at all. But if you aren't consciously seeking improvement, the opportunities for improvement will find you in painful ways. For instance, if you need to learn forgiveness, you'll keep coming across people who hurt you until you learn to forgive.

As I said in the beginning of this book, **your life is all about your choices**. It can be full of happiness and learning, or it could be full of pain and regret.

Actions speak louder than words

It's well and good to want to live a virtuous life, and a different matter entirely to live one. To truly embody your virtues, you need to define actions that help you live them. What does that virtue mean in everyday life?

For example, one of the virtues I want to live is to be mindful and present. Now how do I live it? I consciously breathe deeply whenever I start something—whether it's getting out of bed, stepping into work, before meeting someone, eating, drinking water. That pause, that breath, helps me acknowledge and appreciate the activity I am engaged in. It helps me become aware of how I am feeling and accept those feelings.

Similarly, another character trait I want to embody is self-responsibility. I want to take responsibility for everything that shows up in my life and not blame anyone for it. To do that whenever something triggering happens or when I feel like blaming someone, I pause and think about it. I reaffirm that everything happens for a reason and that reason is there to serve me.

As you start living these actions daily, you'll take big leaps forward in becoming the best version of yourself. And as you change as a person, things in your life will start changing too—you'll start attracting a new reality. Let me tell you a story that I read as a child.

A long, long time ago, there were two querulous women—a mother-in-law and a daughter-in-law—who lived in a town. They were always fighting with each other, complaining bitterly about each other, and finding fault in everything the other one did. The mother-in-law rued her fate and told anyone who would listen, 'what did I do to deserve such a bad daughter-in-law? She doesn't listen to anything I say and always answers back.' The daughter-in-law cried, beat her chest, and told all her friends, 'my mother-in-law is horrible. She doesn't appreciate anything I do and is always complaining.' There were fights every day and both women were deeply unhappy.

One day a saint came to their town and the daughter-in-law decided to go seek his help. 'Guruji, my mother-in-law is making me unhappy. Tell me how to control her; give me some mantra so that I have peace and quiet at home,' she begged the saint.

The wise saint took a bottle of water, closed his eyes, and blew some mantra on the water. He gave the water to the daughter-in-law and said, 'take this is blessed water. The next time your mother-in-law starts complaining, take a big sip of this water and keep it in your mouth. Don't drink it or you'll die. Keep the water in your mouth till your mother-in-law keeps talking, and after that go spit it out and rinse your mouth.'

So, the daughter-in-law did what the saint told her. Now every time her mother-in-law ranted at her, she would take a sip of water and sit with it in her mouth. It was difficult. There were so many times she wanted to respond to her mother-in-law's accusations, but she could not—her mouth was full of water! She didn't dare to drink it or spit it before her mother-in-law calmed down. Who would go against a saint!

Slowly days passed, and her mother-in-law stopped berating her. In fact, she did a complete turnaround. Now she went about telling everyone that she was blessed to have an understanding daughter-in-law. 'No matter how much I complain that sweet girl never says a word,' she told everyone. The daughter-in-law was very happy with this change and both women became much nicer to each other.

A few months later, the same saint came back to town. The daughter-in-law went running to him, 'Guruji, your blessed water is a miracle! I am now so happy, and my mother-in-law has changed completely.'

Smiling the saint said, 'Daughter, the miracle wasn't in the water; it was inside you. I didn't bless the water nor did the water change your mother-in-law. It was all you! When you stopped responding to her comments and complaints, you changed your behaviour. You became a better version of yourself. And when you changed, she changed too.'

All the change we want in our life is within us. Don't wait for your circumstances to change. Take action, change yourself, and your life will automatically change.

A 20-minute morning ritual that can help you move forward on this quest

- Start your day with breathwork and meditation (10 min)

- Visualize the life you want and express gratitude for what you already have (3 min)

- Verbalize or journal positive affirmations for your life (2 min)

- Spend some time feeling connected with nature (5 min)

12 Commandments To Live Your Best Life

1. Understand yourself at a deeper level
2. Overcome limiting thoughts, beliefs, and patterns
3. Live authentically by discovering and pursuing your virtues
4. Heal negative inclinations
5. Release judgements
6. Trust in the universe, release the need to control
7. Speak freely with love
8. Love deeply through acceptance
9. Mindfully engage with everything
10. Be grateful for everything
11. Allow experiences for learning
12. Be patient, compassionate, and tolerant

REFLECTION TIME

DISCOVER

Take the *VIA Survey of Character Strengths* to identify your top five virtues.

www.authentichappiness.sas.upenn.edu/questionnaires/survey-character-strengths

Listen to the *'Guided Visualization to Discover Your Best Self'* online from the Happiness Habits bundle.

What are some character traits that I have built in my life?

_____

_____

_____

_____

DECIDE

In the table below, list down character traits and virtues that would create a paradigm shift in your life. Describe what each of these mean to you and list down actions that will help you make them a habit.

Character trait/ Virtue that is important to me	What does it mean to me? Why is it important to me?	How am I currently suffering as a result of not having enough of this virtue in my life?	How will I put it into action every day?

STRATEGIZE

Download the '*12 Commandments to Live Your Best Life*' from the online Happiness Habits bundle and pin it where you can see it.

Create a morning ritual for yourself:

_____

_____

_____

_____

_____

_____

Purpose: The Invisible Force

Legend says that there was once a prince who led a very sheltered life. He grew up surrounded by riches and had no inkling of human suffering. But he wasn't satisfied with his life in the palace. He had everything he could want, but he still felt that something was missing. So, he stepped out of the confines of the palace to see if the outside world had what he was looking for. As he walked the streets of his kingdom, he was horrified by the suffering he saw. After witnessing this, he couldn't abide by the life in the palace. And so, he left all the riches behind and walked out one night to become a monk. As the legend goes, this prince attained enlightenment under a Bodhi tree and became the Buddha.

As many wise ones have discovered, without purpose and meaning, even a life full of worldly possessions isn't a *happy* life. In his TED talk, Sir Ken Robinson mentioned that he met all kinds of people, most of whom didn't enjoy what they did. They simply got on with their lives and derived no great pleasure from what they did. Instead, they endured it. And then sometimes you meet people who love what they do and couldn't imagine doing anything else. Their work was an extension of themselves. And they were the ones who were truly happy.

In my book, being happy is not just about feeling good. Happiness is different from momentary pleasures. It's deeper and long-lasting. And that kind of happiness stems from having a bigger purpose in life. Your purpose has two important elements:

- Becoming aware of your gifts and bringing them to prominence in your daily life. Becoming more aligned with what you do well.

- Using your skills, beyond just your needs, to contribute to the greater good. That's when you find meaning.

To thrive in life, you need a purpose and meaning. And it doesn't have to be ground-breaking! It doesn't have to be something that changes the world. It could be a smaller, simpler thing that contributes to others in some way. Your purpose is something that gets you going full steam ahead and brings you a sense of joy.

This quest for purpose has been around forever. Everyone seeks it; or if they don't, they feel the lack of it in their lives. Abraham Maslow, the creator of Maslow's Hierarchy of Needs, believed that people always seek fulfilment and change through personal growth—they are always changing and growing. He defined five stages of needs, starting from basic physiological needs necessary for survival to the topmost self-actualization needs that are fuelled by the desire to be all that one can be. This top level is the pursuit of purpose.

All of us have a purpose. Some of us are lucky and we know what it is. But more often than not it's hidden in plain sight or hindered by our unmet lower-level needs such as food, shelter, connection, etc. If you are worried about where your next meal is coming from, you are probably not thinking about the higher purpose of your life!

If you are reading this book, there is a strong chance that your survival and safety needs have been met and now you are in a quest to figure out, 'What next?' This is the time when questions like 'What am I doing?' 'Why am I doing this?' 'Is it even important to me?' start rearing their heads.

Once you start thinking about it, you'll realize that your purpose was there with you all along. It's effectively about being your best self and doing what you love to do. It's about bringing your best gifts to the fore and making them a part of your daily life. And your gifts have been with you, even though they might be unexpressed. It could be a hobby at the moment. It could be something that people keep coming to you for. It could be something creative. Or a gift for being a speaker, coach, or mentor.

If you don't know what your purpose is, it's because you've not really looked for it, or that you've just gone with whatever direction that life has taken you and never bothered to become aware of 'what it is that you are good at', 'what is it that you want to do', etc.

Your purpose is unique

When I was researching content for this book, I came across a story on medium[14] that I am reproducing, as is, here.

Peter Parrot came home upset and confused.

'What's wrong?' his mother asked.

'I hate my stupid beak!' Peter blurted.

'Why do you hate your beak? I think it's beautiful,' his mother said reassuringly.

'All of the other birds have much cooler beaks. Sammy Spoonbill, Pammy Pelican, Harry Hawk, Freddy Finch, all of them!'

Peter's mother sat silently for a moment. 'He may be right,' she thought to herself, they do have very cool beaks.

---

14. This story belongs to https://medium.com/small-motivational-stories/the-jealous-parrot-50bb8f728b3f

'You should go and see Major Macaw; he'll know what to do. He's the wisest of the parrots and lives in the tallest tree in the forest. Yes, he'll know what to do,' responded Peter's mother.

So, Peter Parrot flew to the tallest tree in the forest and found Major Macaw.

'Excuse me Major, I have a problem,' said Peter.

'Oh dear, what can it be?' asked the venerable macaw.

'I have a stupid beak. Why can't I have a cool beak like Sammy Spoonbill, Pammy Pelican, Harry Hawk or Freddy Finch?'

'You're right.' said the macaw, 'They do have cool beaks. Tell me Peter, do you like eating worms and crustaceans?'

'Yuck! That would be disgusting!' responded Peter.

'Well, that's what the spoonbill's beak is designed for. What about fish?'

'I couldn't think of anything worse,' said Peter.

'So, the pelican's beak would not work either.'

'What about rabbits and mice?'

'Eww.'

'OK, so maybe you shouldn't aspire to have a hawk's beak. Small seeds?'

'They're not so bad, but my favourite is Brazil nuts.' exclaimed Peter, salivating at the thought.

'That's lucky, I think I have a few here. Would you like one?' asked Major.

Peter's eyes lit up. 'Yes, please.'

'Tell me Peter, if you had the beak of a spoonbill, pelican, hawk or finch, do you think that you could eat that Brazil nut?'

'I guess not,' said Peter with his mouth full.

'You see, young parrot, you have been designed a certain way, with certain skills, attributes and tastes. Don't waste your life being envious of the capacities of others, just make sure that you know what you're good at and why you're here.'

Peter nodded his head in understanding and flew back home much more content.

Your skills and capabilities may be very different from what you see around you, but trust that they are uniquely suited to your purpose. So, don't bother about what others are doing; instead, focus on what brings you meaning and joy.

Discovering your purpose

How do you go about discovering your purpose then? A simple and widely used approach is *Ikigai*—the Japanese concept of finding purpose in life. Ikigai is the sweet spot at the intersection of four main elements—what you love to do, what you are good at, what the world needs, and what you can be paid for (remember survival!).

Of course, even if the first three conditions are met—what you love to do, what you are good at, and what the world needs—you have a handle on your purpose. The 'getting paid' part is a bonus, but not a necessity. You can still make your money elsewhere while pursuing your purpose for the sheer joy of it.

The key is to get very, very specific. So, it's not enough to say 'I love music' or photography or cooking or coaching. You have to think deeper. For instance, as a coach, what could be your gift? Are you a great listener? Can you get the meaning behind the words that are being spoken? Are you a great people-person, able to put anyone at ease?

Here's how you go about testing whether it's a gift that is meant to be your purpose:

- It is something that's been with you for a long time in some form or the other.

- You are truly interested in it.

- You know that you're good at it, and if you are able to bring that gift out, you will stand out from the crowd.

- Once you are aware of a gift, you would be more motivated to use it regularly—finding more happiness as you do so.

To consistently pursue your purpose, you need to set a direction—where you want to go with it. You want to set goals in a certain format so that you are able to direct yourself in a way that you move towards an optimistic future. However, even after you discover your purpose, it might not be so easy to follow it. That's where motivation comes in.

Motivation: moving ahead on the quest of purpose

For most of us, living our purpose is a journey. Finding your purpose and living it does not just happen one fine day as you wake up. You have to make space for it in the life that you are living, and you have to find constant motivation for it to do so. Motivation is your ability to sustain a higher level of energy and investment in anything that you do. The lack of motivation shows up as apathy and the lack of energy to get anything done. One of the drivers of happiness is your ability to complete things, to make progress, to move forward, and to express your best self—all of these require you to be motivated.

'But if your purpose is what you so enjoy doing, won't you be motivated to follow it anyway?' said Neuro, my ever-present reality check.

It's true that the more you are in alignment with your purpose, the more you are motivated. But other aspects of life can pull you down and demotivate you. Think of entrepreneurs. These are people who have found their passion and followed it through. But have you ever heard of entrepreneur burnout? If they become too engrossed in what they are doing and don't pay attention to their health or mental wellbeing, they start getting tired, making the wrong decisions, and feeling that nothing is going right. In that situation, it feels really difficult to get out there and do the thing you love—because you've lost the balance in your life. So, while purpose is important, it is still just one of the quests to happiness—and the others need equal attention too!

Coming back to the aspect of motivation. Most of us are in a place in life where we do things because of a need. While you're trying to figure out who you are, you still have a day-to-day life that you have to live. That is where most of us struggle to find motivation.

In reality, while there is an aspirational future that we would attempt to arrive at, and while we have goals that we want to achieve, there is a struggle that we face today which leads to different levels of motivation. Some of us are completely demotivated, some of us are highly motivated, and there is a huge bunch of people who are in the middle.

How to deal with this lack of motivation while you try to figure out your purpose?

The *first step is to identify where your motivation comes from*. Is it from an external driver like trying to avoid punishment or earn a reward? Or is it something that stems from your inner drive, your sense of purpose, and your enjoyment of the activity itself?

No prizes for guessing, but motivation that comes from within is what drives long-term, sustained happiness.

The *second step is to identify what motivates you*. There are several drivers of motivation. You could be driven by status, acceptance, freedom, mastery, curiosity, power, honour, or any number of things. Take an honest assessment of your motivators at the end of this chapter.

Here's the catch. You will always find yourself moving up and down on the motivation spectrum. Sometimes, you'll be on a high and at other times, you will feel low. The secret that happy people are privy to is to catch yourself before you fall all the way down to demotivation.

Demotivation can manifest in many ways. You could feel lethargic and lazy; start procrastinating, slipping up on your game, and making errors in judgment; or begin to feel like a victim of circumstances, like you have to do some things or tolerate the situation, etc. The trick is in identifying the early signs of demotivation and taking action to overcome them.

If, on the other hand, you let yourself be completely demotivated, you will either drop the plan altogether or find it a very difficult climb uphill to find your motivation again—it'll sap your energy!

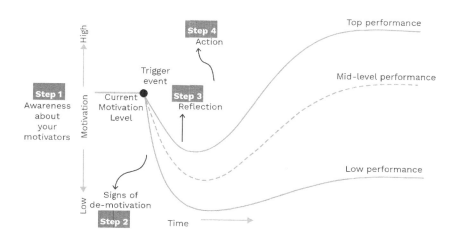

As an urban working professional, your happiness is tied to your work conditions. You likely spend a significant amount of time at work, interacting with your colleagues and dealing with ever-changing situations at work. What happens in the workplace spills over in the other areas of life as well. So, if things aren't going well there, your overall happiness will be affected. And work is also the main showcase of your skills, right? Which, in itself, is a significant aspect of your happiness. But often these may not align.

Many of us are not yet in the zone or position where we can live our purpose in full. We'd like to get there eventually, but, for now, we need to improve our current situation in life. Most people are in that zone where there is a varying degree of dissatisfaction with where they are. And that's exactly what happened to me.

I've always known that my purpose is to share ideas through speaking, teaching, coaching, or writing. This is what I wanted to do. However, as an HR in a corporate setting, this is not what I did in my everyday work-life. And I always felt a sense of dissatisfaction. Finally, that dissatisfaction started changing to demotivation. I felt nothing challenged me anymore and work had just become a routine. I was unhappy and had no energy to do anything.

And so, I decided to actively pursue my purpose. I couldn't leave my job because I needed that financial stability, but I could take some time out to do what I loved. I started monthly coaching sessions at work covering various topics. I started redirecting myself to more reading, learning, and researching for this one-hour intense session. Attendance grew over time, and I found myself enjoying these sessions. This expression of what I was good at made me feel alive, and that feeling percolated into other aspects of my life as well.

I found that just by taking time out to do this one session, I was able to find a lot more energy and motivation for other things as well. That apathy I had fallen into vanished! Even my job found a new meaning— as a financier of my purpose.

This led me to an interesting realization. When you pursue your purpose, it's not always about having to give up your current livelihood. That's the greatest fear of most people. How can they leave financial stability and ride off into the sunset after their purpose? And because of that fear, most people do nothing.

But it's not a zero-sum game. It's not all or nothing. It's not black or white. There is no need for conflict.

Your purpose can coexist with your other responsibilities. It took me a while to figure it out, but I realized I could coach even as I did other work that paid my bills. At some point, when everything aligns, you can go do what you love full-time.

Over time I expanded my coaching footprint. I would coach for free because my job allowed me financial freedom. I would informally coach ex-colleagues, friends, and family over weekends. It allowed me to fine-tune my skill. It allowed me to feel happy about the contribution that I was making. And because I was able to do those things, it gave me a much better acceptance of my current job.

I went from, 'I just have to get out of this rat race,' to 'this job is paying me not only to have a good life, but also allowing me to do things that I love.'

And that shift made all the difference. There is nothing holding you back from pursuing your purpose. The conflict, the conundrum, the restriction is all in your own mind. Think beyond your fears and see what you can do ***today*** to go after what you love doing!

Don't hold back

The quest for purpose is not an easy road. Even if you do know your purpose, you'll still struggle to follow that path. Sometimes, as we saw earlier, life gets in the way. Sometimes, we have self-belief issues and don't trust our own abilities. Sometimes, societal conditioning, limiting beliefs, money blocks, or any number of obstacles show up. It can be really, really hard in the face of these obstacles to stay true to your purpose and try to live it every day. This is why motivation is such a big factor in this quest.

Find your purpose

Some people just know their purpose, and for some of us, it takes a bit of work to find it. So, don't worry if you don't have a clear purpose yet. That fulfilment and meaning could be just around the corner. For now, focus on finding it. Here's how you can do it:

1. Clear away all distractions and relax yourself.

2. Make a list of everything you do right now. Circle everything that gives you meaning and fulfilment, and cross out those that don't.

3. Think about things that have given you fulfilment and meaning in the past. Write them down and compare them to your list in point 2.

4. Think about the times you have suffered in life. Suffering often is the path to deeper meaning and most people find their purpose after going through life-changing experiences.

5. Listen to your consciousness and your heart. Spend time in silence, take a walk, meditate. The answers will come to you.

6. Learn from others and find inspiration. What are people saying that feels meaningful? What resonates with you?

7. Take action. You won't find your purpose by just thinking about it. So, go out and do what feels right.

How to live a life of purpose

Living your purpose is not something that happens overnight. It's not always simple to live a life of purpose and neither is there a formula to it. What I can do is give you some pointers that have helped me in my quest for purpose.

1. Create some guiding principles for yourself and keep adding to them. These are not set in stone but are values that resonate with you and will guide you well. Make a list and keep it where you can see it every day. Maybe create a happiness vision board and add it to that. Try and live by these principles as much as you can, evolving them as you grow.

2. Don't lose sight of your purpose. Reflect on it every day. 'How am I living my purpose? What can I do today to serve my purpose?'

3. Do everything with purpose. Setting an intention for every task will help you find more meaning in it. Be it anything that you are doing—writing, coaching, speaking—set an intention to serve.

4. Keep yourself on track. It's easy to fall back into old patterns and get distracted from your purpose. Keep reviewing yourself on this quest. Take a few minutes every day to ask yourself, 'How have I lived my purpose today? What is going well and what can I do better?' Reflect on it, and if it helps, write it down. Be consistent with these reviews.

5. Get accountability partners. Find people who will support your journey, who care about you and what you are doing. Find people who will hold you accountable and maybe even support your purpose in some way.

6. Don't go through the motions. You have to feel your purpose and find joy in acting on it. If it isn't connecting with you on a deeper level, then maybe you are barking up the wrong tree.

It's not always about the big things

While you are seeking your purpose, don't stop living life as it comes to you. Purpose and meaning are not always about the big things or one grand idea. You can engage with everyday life meaningfully. In everything you do, there is a chance to express your best self and experience it fully. You don't always have to quit your job and go on a great adventure. You can find meaning and fulfilment right where you are, in micro-moments of positive contributions.

REFLECTION TIME

DISCOVER

Find your Ikigai or your purpose using this template:

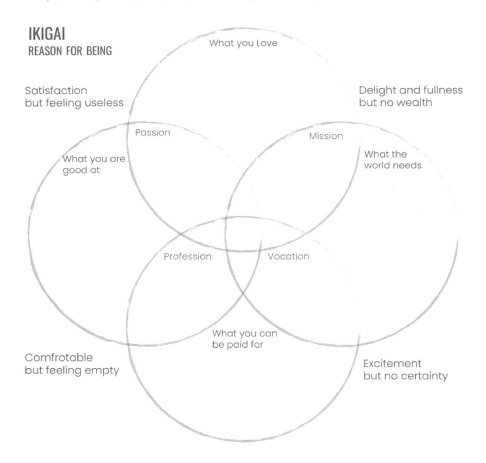

IKIGAI
REASON FOR BEING

What you Love

Satisfaction
but feeling useless

Delight and fullness
but no wealth

Passion

Mission

What you are
good at

What the
world needs

Profession

Vocation

What you can
be paid for

Comfrotable
but feeling empty

Excitement
but no certainty

Take the *'Software Code That Runs You'* assessment on *www. happinesshabits.in* to find out how your life aligns with your purpose.

Rank your motivators in order of preference.

Motivator	What it means	Rank
Status	My position is good, and recognized by the people who work with me	
Acceptance	The people around me approve of what I do and who I am	
Freedom	I am independent of others with my work and my responsibilities	
Mastery	My work challenges my competence, but it is still within my abilities	
Purpose	My purpose in life is reflected in the work that I do	
Order	There are enough rules and policies for a stable environment	
Curiosity	I have plenty of things to investigate and to think about	
Relatedness	I have good social contacts	
Power	There is enough room for me to influence what happens around me	
Honour	I feel proud that my personal values are reflected in what I do	
Other		

What are the events or triggers that make me feel demotivated?

_____

_____

_____

_____

_____

_____

_____

DECIDE

In the Discover section, you ranked your motivators. Now, let us explore how they can contribute to discovering your purpose.

What can I do today to pursue my purpose?

_____

_____

_____

_____

_____

_____

STRATEGIZE

Reflect on the inputs you got from Ikigai, assessment, your motivators and triggers for demotivation. Note down the insights you received from them.

_____

_____

_____

_____

_____

_____

Sit in silence for a few minutes and ask yourself:

What can I do today to be more in alignment with my true purpose?

_____

_____

_____

_____

_____

_____

Based on these inputs, take small baby steps to live your purpose.

For example, if an input directs you to follow your passion in music, then see what is the small thing that you can do to follow that. Invest one hour over the weekend to create something around your passion or to practise something.

What are the small steps I can take to live my purpose?

_____

_____

_____

_____

_____

Practice 'keeping your word' to yourself and others—DO what you say you will do.

Learn to tap into your Sid—quieten the noise in your head and listen to what your 'silent watcher' voice has to say.

Be patient.

A Balanced Life

Research shows that dreams are important in helping us sort through our memories, emotions, and complex thoughts. Maybe that's why Sid played such a big role in my discovery of happiness. He made it easier to sort through the chaos and focus on what's important. He zeroed in on the things that I was missing out on. And he helped me learn the lessons that were within my reach but side-lined in reality. One such lesson he taught me was about balance.

I found myself sitting on a park bench with Sid perched near my shoulder. We were surrounded by greenery and the melodious sounds of birds chirping. A little ahead, some ducks were swimming in a lake. It was an idyllic setting for some romance! But here I was, with Sid!

Just as the thought crossed my mind, the all-wise raven piped up, 'what? Am I not good enough for you? Shall we move to a desert instead?'

'All right, all right, don't ruffle your feathers,' I smiled at him. 'Tell me, what's on the cards today? Why are we here?'

'Well, if you insist.' I swear that raven sniffed at me! 'Today, you get to see two pretty cool things,' he added.

'First things first,' Sid announced, as if giving a lecture, 'did you know your outside is a reflection of your inside?'

I grinned at him, 'I only know of a local gambling game called *In and Out*. Have you taken up gambling, Sid?' I asked innocently.

'Always the smartass,' grumbled Sid. 'This is serious life-altering stuff we are talking about! Quit fooling around,' he scolded.

'Now, listen carefully,' he continued, 'All these problems areas in life that you worry about are nothing but clues to solve a puzzle. They aren't here to cause you unhappiness; rather, they are the key to unlocking the next level of YOU in the quest for sustained happiness.'

'I don't understand,' I replied.

'Think about it this way,' explained Sid, 'Let's say, there is a person you frequently get into a disagreement with—maybe your spouse. They aren't here to heckle you; they are here to teach you. In fact, before you came on to this planet you might have asked them to behave that way to help you evolve. If they are doing something that you asked them to do in the first place—to help you learn a lesson that would move you closer to nirvana—how can that be bad? You find that annoying because you can't see what's underneath—the true intention. Uncovering this true intention is your job. If you have a tough coach trying to help you learn something that will improve your skills, will you fire the coach or will you thank the coach for doing a great job?'

'That sounds really complicated,' I said. 'How can I figure out what I asked someone to do before I even got here? Won't I just be looking for a deeper meaning in everything? I don't have the time for that!'

'It's not that difficult when you know what to look for,' replied Sid. 'Happiness is about balance in all aspects of life. When something in your life is not balanced, it cries for attention. That is its way of telling you that it's your next clue. If you try to push it away, it cries harder, it becomes more persistent.'

'Okay,' I said, trying to digest this information. 'My problems are here to help me! Who would have thought!'

Sid tapped me with his beak to get my attention again, 'Now, for the second lesson of the day; you know these guided missiles that lock on a target ... the ones that can follow the target even when it shifts and hit it, right?'

I looked at him, wondering where he is going with that, and replied, 'Yes I do. Quite handy for destruction, they are.'

Sid gave me a look and continued, 'Well, the point is not destruction, but the lock on the target. Like the missile, you also have a guiding system. It's called the RAS—Reticular Activating System.'

As I failed to imagine myself as a weapon of mass destruction, I get ready to interrupt Sid. Anticipating this, he continued with his voice just a tad bit higher, 'When you make something your goal or priority and make that absolutely clear in your mind, you lock on the target, in a way. The RAS is like a heat signature or a sniffer dog that picks up relevant information related to that goal and magnifies it for you. In the myriad quantum of details that hit us, these relevant ones get tagged. Which is why if you have decided to buy a *red* Range Rover Evoque, you will suddenly start seeing more of those cars on the road. Do you think more people have started buying it because you like that colour? Of course, not! The cars were always there, they just didn't make it past your brain filters. But now that it's a priority for you, the RAS is on your side and is trying to make it a reality.'

'That is seriously cool,' I replied, in awe.

'If you are done gushing, can we focus on understanding the utility and power of this system?' groused Sid (seriously! What have I done to deserve a grumpy, snarky spirit guide!)?

Oblivious to my musings, Sid continued, 'RAS is your ally in making your goals a reality. Of course, you need to take the required actions, but if you use the RAS effectively, you can reach your goals faster.'

And with that he flew off, leaving me to chew on everything he had said.

Finding balance

When I had my first child, my world turned upside down. As a new parent, everything in my life changed. This tiny human was the priority and everything else—work, friendships, health, and wellbeing—took a backseat. It was overwhelming and I didn't know what to make of it. Both my wife and I struggled to make the most of this new reality we found ourselves in. Parenting was a new dimension added to our life and we didn't know how to balance it against everything else.

I'd realize much later that I was struggling for perfection. I wanted to do 100% of everything at all times. And life is just not meant to be lived that way. We are only human after all.

Instead of perfection, what we need is balance.

Most of us try to compartmentalize our lives—this is personal, this is work, this is relationship, and so on. What we forget is that we are one person, and whatever is happening in one area of our life, is bound to affect the other.

If you are dealing with grief or loss in your personal life, can you focus on work? Can you pay attention to your health and wellbeing? If you are having a career crisis, can you give your 100% to your relationships? No! If something is not working in one area of your life, it is bound to affect everything else and degrade all these aspects.

Here's one of the most common mistakes people end up making— working too hard for money. What's the point of that money if overwork causes you to burnout? What if the stress gives you a heart attack?! I don't want to be morbid, but I do want you to really understand that to live a happy life, you need to live well in everything that it entails.

And don't give yourself the excuse that you are 'doing it all for the family', either. What good is working yourself to death if your family doesn't get to spend time with you?

If you choose to push yourself harder on a particular aspect of life, that is because you are pursuing your own compulsions. And whether you know it right now or not, it is making you unhappy.

Happiness comes from finding balance in things that are important to you in life. And no one can tell you what these things are. You have to decide for yourself.

Prioritize what's important to you

My daughter shared this thought with me and today, I'd like to share it with you.

'Imagine you had a bank account. Every morning, Rs 86,400 were deposited in the account. But the condition was that the account could not carry over any balance. You could not keep what you had yesterday, and anything that you did not spend today was removed from the account. If you had an account like that, what would you do? Make use of every rupee in it right?

Well, we all have such an account—it's Time. Every morning, it credits you with 86,400 seconds. Every night it writes off whatever time you have failed to use wisely. You can't use more than you have, and every day, the account starts afresh. You can't get back lost time.

Isn't every second precious, then? Why not use the time you have to do the things that you want to do? You have more than enough time if you channel it well and know your priorities.'

Balance is only possible when you allow room for negotiation. Life is never constant. At different points in your life, you want different things. Your priorities change as your life circumstances change. For example, when I became a father, my priority was my child—work, social relationships, etc., had to take a back seat to that.

Negotiation is about understanding what you need, desire, and require more at that point in life, and figuring out what dimensions you can dial down on, for a while.

Now, this does not mean dial down permanently! If you get too immersed in your role as a parent, you'll soon start missing your social interactions and that will make you unhappy. Negotiation is about saying, 'okay, I went out and met my friends and relatives three days a week. Now that I am a father, I can only do that once a week, and sometimes, just once in 15 days. I will get back to my usual level of social interaction in a few years when my child grows up.'

Balance is not about cutting yourself off entirely. It's about thinking through your priorities in the short term and making conscious choices about what you need to be happy.

So, if your social dimension was at a 9 or 10 before you became a parent, you could negotiate and keep it at a 5 now. But make sure it doesn't go to 0; because your lack of social expression will then frustrate you!

Every dimension in life—health, wealth, relationships, career, parenting, social, spiritual, and self-care—needs to maintain a certain threshold level. The key is in balancing different life aspects in a way that your current situation determines the priorities that you want to deal with.

For instance, if you are at a critical point in your career, you may not spend two hours in the gym every day. But that also does not mean that you can ignore your health entirely. Similarly, if you don't spend enough 'me-time' doing things you like to do, then you won't be able to unwind, and that stress will spread to all the other dimensions.

Remember, everything in life is interlinked. You cannot neglect some areas and still expect happiness. When you move the entire system within yourself forward, you inch closer to the real state of happiness.

But balance isn't that difficult to achieve. It's not about mega life-changing decisions. Rather, balance is about the little things to strive for, every day. Let's see how that works across a few dimensions:

1. **Health**

   One of the most difficult things people struggle with when it comes to physical wellbeing is eating healthy. The challenge is that we try to stop eating junk. Instead, if you focus more on eating the good stuff, you won't have space for the junk. It's a simple shift and far easier to implement than abstaining entirely. For example, just adding a glass of green juice to your daily diet could do a world of good.

   Similarly, for your mental wellbeing, you don't have to spend hours meditating. Just walk barefoot on grass or unpaved ground or sit outside in the morning sunlight as you read a paper. It's the little things that add up to make a big difference.

2. **Relationships**

   Take your relationship with your spouse, for instance. In his book *Five Languages of Love*, Gary Chapman talks about how different people expect different kinds of love. Some people like something gifted to them, some like words, others like touch, etc. So, if you and your partner belong to different categories, there will always be a conflict even though there is no fundamental drift, per say. You get into trouble just because of the way you express love. The idea is to figure out what works for you. Set aside date nights, leave each other notes of appreciation, take up some of their responsibilities and give them a breather—small things can go a long way to strengthen your relationship.

   Another thing to improve relationships is to love unconditionally—be it your spouse, parents, children, friends, or anyone else. Unfortunately, our concept of love is very conditional. We treat it almost like a transaction, 'do this and you'll be loved, else you won't.' Conditional love leeches away happiness. Learn to give and receive love unconditionally and see your relationships bloom.

3. **Self-care**

You can't pour from an empty cup. To practise to the best of your abilities, you need time to do things that de-stress and re-energize you. For some people, it could just be a walk, spending time with a hobby like gardening, or an evening listening to music and just relaxing without thinking about anything. Just make sure to take that time out and do what you need!

Setting goals that matter and making happiness a reality

There are two powerful tools that are going to help you in this quest—visualization and vision boarding.

Visualization is a mental picture you make of the things you want in life—your goals. This is the technique that activates your Reticular Activating System (RAS) and focuses it on your goals. But just a mental picture is not enough, you have to bring in the *feeling*. How would you feel once you meet that goal? That's what triggers the RAS. For example, if your goal is to buy a new car, just having a mental image of the car is not enough. You have to visualize how you will feel while driving this car. If you want a promotion, then just seeing yourself in the new role is not enough. You have to visualize how you'll feel once you are promoted. The idea is to think about these goals as if they have already happened—and they will!

Vision boarding is also a way to put what you want right in front of your eyes. It's a great tool for people who have trouble visualizing, because it makes the future very tangible. A vision board could be anything—pictures that show your goals, quotes that resonate with you, even elements of touch and smell! Just stick them on a pinboard and keep it where you see it every day. The idea is to keep that future in a clear line of sight, so that you are able to choose actions that propel you in the direction of your goals.

But these are just tools that aid focus. The real power lies within you—your mind. These tools won't work if your mental blocks are obstructing your way.

'*I want this, but I don't deserve it.*'

'*How can I have this? I have not worked hard enough for it.*'

Sounds familiar?

These limiting beliefs block your intentions and tell your subconscious that the desire isn't important enough. You don't believe you can make it happen. In that case, the visualization or vision board just becomes a picture with no real power to it.

It's totally possible to work around these blocks. You can overcome them with the quest to become a better version of yourself, or you can work on healing them. You can use simple techniques like daily affirmations to overcome the limiting beliefs and implant new, more positive beliefs. To do that, you need clarity.

Take some time to think about the blueprint of your life. The important question is, 'What do I want?' Once you have a handle on that, create short-term goals. 'How can I achieve this in the next six months, one year, two years?'

When you are setting your goals, don't be limited by just what *you* want. Think about how you can stretch that goal beyond yourself. Figure out how your efforts in any dimension can benefit others—your team, family, spouse, or even humanity! For example, if your goal is to be at the peak of your health, is it just because it makes you look and feel good? Or can you leverage health in other dimensions of life? For example, if I am fitter, I can run around and play with my daughter who is a super-active eight-year-old. Similarly, if your goal is wealth, what can you do to use that wealth for the betterment of others?

When you have your goals, create a daily plan of action. 'What can I do every day that will take me closer to my goals?' Then, monitor the progress. 'Is everything going as it should?'

Remember, happiness is in the details!

Keeping on the right path

I'm sure that, by now, you know that if something isn't working out despite all your efforts, then it's the universe's way of telling you, 'you are on the wrong path, buddy.'

If you are constantly getting stuck in some dimension—relationship, money, career—then you need to re-look at what you are doing and why. This is a message for you to work deeper on some aspect of yourself to bring it in alignment with your soul's purpose.

REFLECTION TIME

DISCOVER

In each of the life dimensions below, figure out what your priorities are, where you currently are, and where you would want to be in the next few years.

Life Dimensions	Priorities	Current state	Desired state
Health			
Wealth			
Relationship			
Career			
Parenting			
Social			
Spiritual			
Self-care			

DECIDE

For each of these priorities, make a plan on how you are going to achieve your desired state.

Life Dimensions	Priorities	Action Plan
Health		
Wealth		
Relationship		
Career		
Parenting		
Social		
Spiritual		
Self-care		

STRATEGIZE

What are some challenges that might derail me? What can I do to overcome these challenges?

Challenge	How will I overcome it?

Emotional Mastery

You went to ask your colleague for some input about a project you both are working on and were rudely rebuffed. It made you angry.

You are late for work, and someone cuts in ahead of you in traffic. You are irritated.

You are relaxing at home, finally sitting down to do something you enjoy, and your spouse now wants you to help out with something. You are annoyed.

Sounds familiar?

We all have an emotional response to triggers that come at us several times a day. Emotions influence how we live and interact with each other, and they have a direct effect on our bodies, relationships, and work.

- **Body:** Negative attitudes and feelings of helplessness and hopelessness can create chronic stress. This upsets the body's hormone balance, depletes the brain chemicals required for happiness, and damages the immune system.

- **Relationships:** Emotional build-up over time can result in an emotional outburst, which affects your relationships.

- **Work:** People are not isolated 'emotional islands[15]'. Your moods, emotions, and overall dispositions have an impact on job performance, decision making, creativity, turnover, teamwork, negotiations, and leadership.

Our choices, actions, and perceptions are all influenced by the emotions we experience at any given moment. These are all key ingredients of happiness! And so, our happiness is closely linked to our emotions.

Emotional Mastery is the ability to exercise control over your emotional state and channelling it in a more constructive direction. It's not about suppressing your emotions. It's about acknowledging and accepting them—a tough feat in the times we live in.

---

15. https://www.managementtoday.co.uk/emotional-workplace/article/652015

Today, we live in a constant state of stress; it's our default state. The worst bit is that we are not even aware of it! We are stressed about our jobs, relationships, money, health—you name it. There's always the pressure to do the next thing. There's always something pending, something not done.

Stress, if not released, has an adverse effect on us physically, mentally, and emotionally. There is enough and more evidence to support the relationship of lifestyle diseases[16] such as obesity, diabetes, and heart conditions to stress. In response to stress[17], your body releases the stress hormone—cortisol—which leads to fatigue, high blood pressure, and irritability. It's a vicious cycle. If you are not physically in sound health, you tend to be more stressed about things, and that, in turn, feeds back into damaging your health. While the physical signs of stress are visible, its impact on your happiness and wellbeing is not that visible—and often missed.

As I write this book, COVID-19 has blocked our avenues for releasing stress, like going to the gym, shopping, meeting friends, etc. So, it has been building up. Added to that, there is a genuinely heightened fear of death, fear of the future, fear of what will happen, fear of losing loved ones. And it's not something that is going away; it's constantly been in the background. You're not thinking about it every minute, but in the back of your head, you're worried. You're also in a limbo. COVID-19 has also taken away one of our fundamental needs to have some level of control over our environment and our future. You can't think of the future because you don't know what it is going to be like. You can't plan for anything that you celebrated or were a part of. Your life is just stuck in a place. And now, with this sense of control completely gone out the window, you have heightened anxiety and stress.

Stress creates an emotional response that, if not managed well, can lead you to make decisions and take actions that take you away from the happiness you desire.

There is a story in the Mahabharata. Once, the five Pandava brothers went hunting in the forest with Sri Krishna. By the time they were done with the hunt, it was almost dusk. Realizing that they wouldn't make it back to the

---

16. https://www.webmd.com/balance/stress-management/features/10-fixable-stress-related-health-problems

17. https://www.healthline.com/health/high-cortisol-symptoms#symptoms

kingdom before the sun goes down, the Pandavas decided to spend the night in the forest. In search of a camping site, they found a cave. It was agreed that each person would stand guard for two hours while the others slept.

The youngest brother, Sahadeva, took the first watch. He sat at the entrance of the cave, holding all his weapons aloft as the others went to sleep inside. As an hour and a half passed, Sahadeva noticed someone approaching him from a distance.

'Stop!' Sahadeva bellowed, 'Who are you? Where are you going?'

The dwarf stopped in his tracks. He said, 'As you can see, I am a tiny dwarf. I want to fight you.' Sahadeva was amused. He thought, 'Here I am, a six-footer. And this foot-and-a-half tall dwarf is challenging me. This is not even a contest!'

For the sake of entertainment, the young Pandava agreed to fight the dwarf. Little did he know that the person he was facing was no ordinary dwarf.

The mysterious stranger defeated Sahadeva with ease, and then tied him up with a rope, left him on the ground, and disappeared into the nearby foliage.

In a while, Nakula woke up and came out of the cave. He found Sahadeva missing from his post. As Nakula called out to his younger brother, a faint voice replied, 'I am here.'

Seeing Sahadeva tied up, Nakula inquired, 'Who did this to you, brother?' Sahadeva could not bring himself to say that he had lost to a tiny dwarf. Instead, he replied, 'I just felt like tying myself up and resting on the ground.'

After freeing his brother, Nakula said, 'Okay, go and get some rest now; I will keep watch.'

Just before Nakula's two hours came to a close, the dwarf re-appeared and challenged him for a fight. Nakula ended up just like his brother did—defeated and tied up.

Soon, Arjuna followed suit. All the brothers faced the same situation, including the indomitable Bhima and the wise Yudhishthira.

Finally, it was Krishna's turn. He appeared from the cave and found the eldest of the Pandavas on the ground. As he freed Yudhishthira, Krishna asked him what had happened.

Yudhishthira always spoke the truth. He told Krishna the entire story.

'I don't understand what happened,' he recounted, 'When my watch was just about to end, this tiny dwarf appeared from nowhere and said, "I want to wrestle you." When we began the bout, something strange happened. The more I fought, the bigger the dwarf became. Soon, he was a huge giant, and I was like a child before him. He caught hold of me with ease, threw me on the ground, and tied me up!'

Krishna smiled and said, 'Never mind. Go and rest. Now that I am awake, I will see to him.' Just as dawn was about to break, Krishna saw the dwarf walking towards him. When he reached closer, Krishna asked, 'What brings you here?' The dwarf replied, 'I want to wrestle and defeat you.'

Krishna accepted the challenge and prepared himself. As soon as both of them began to wrestle each other, the dwarf started to grow in size.

Right then, with a light smile on his face, Krishna threw down his weapons. He sat on the ground and announced, 'You can hit me.' With every blow Krishna received, the dwarf began to shrink. Soon, when he got too tiny, Krishna tied him up in his pitambari (Krishna's customary yellow wrap).

By dawn, the brothers woke up and came out of the cave. Seeing Krishna at his post, they asked, 'Did someone come to see you while you stood guard?' Krishna replied, 'Ah yes, a tiny dwarf came to fight me.'

'So, what did you do with him?'

'I did nothing. Here he is, tied up in my pitambari,' Krishna replied, as he held up his wound-up wrap.

This took the Pandavas by surprise. They exclaimed, 'What is the meaning of this? When we fought him, he continued to grow stronger. And yet here he is, tied up in your wrap!'

With a smile, Krishna revealed the true identity of the dwarf to the Pandavas. It was none other than anger.

He explained, 'Anger assumed the form of a dwarf and fought you. The more you fought the anger before you, the more the anger within you grew. This made the anger confronting you bigger and bigger until it became so huge that it overpowered you and tied you to the ground.' Yudhishthira said, 'I understand now. You were the only one who *recognized him. When you did not express anger in return, he became so small that he was insignificant.'*

This story signifies that negative qualities will always exist. If you try to remove them from your life, you will end up in a fight which you are bound to lose. The more you struggle, the stronger they become. All you have to do is simply ignore them and focus on adopting positive qualities, tendencies, actions and behaviours in your life. The negativities will go away on their own; they will become mute.

Most of us, overwhelmed with emotion, act first and think later. All of us have done so at some point in time. But these decisions, especially those influenced by emotions like fear, anger, jealousy, etc., are not always in our best interests. They lead to destructive outcomes instead of constructive ones.

Here, I want to highlight an important distinction. By itself, no emotion is positive or negative. It's only when they become extreme that all emotions can lead to negative outcomes. Some anger is good if it allows you to take constructive action. Emotional mastery is about constructive versus destructive outcomes more than choosing the so-called positive emotions over negative ones.

Here's how our emotional response pans out:

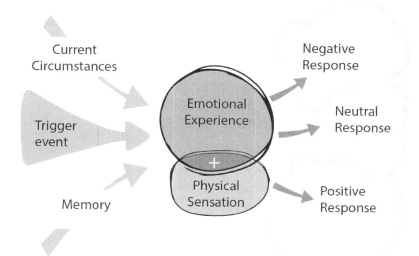

Let's say, you are going about your day, and you encounter an external trigger. Remember the three scenarios I started with? Those are triggers. *A trigger, combined with your current circumstance and past experiences, creates an emotional experience*. This emotional experience can sometimes also be accompanied by a physical response. This emotional experience pushes you to give a response to the trigger. This is where emotional mastery comes in. *If you are aware of your emotional state—how you feel at the moment—and can direct it, you can respond to the trigger neutrally or constructively.* However, if you don't have emotional mastery, your response would be destructive and not good for your own peace of mind and happiness.

Let's look at an example of this—say, a bad day in general. That's something we are all familiar with, right? Let's say, you were juggling multiple deadlines and didn't sleep well the night before. You wake up groggy and not in the best of moods. Then you get caught up in traffic, and someone cuts you off. That's a trigger. You get angry and shout at the person. By this time, cortisol is flooding your system. You arrive at work tired and irritable. It's already becoming a chain reaction of negative events. On top of that, in the middle of a presentation, someone rudely disagrees with you. You are reminded of a bully, and you feel attacked and angry. Your heart rate goes up, and your jaw clenches. You want nothing more than to put that person down! You argue back and belittle the person. They don't like it, and it triggers a whole different chain of events that isn't going to go very well. By now, your day is pretty much destroyed. You go home in a huff and snap at your family. Everyone is upset and unhappy.

What made your day go down the drain was your response to the triggers that came your way. In a constantly stressed state, we tend to interpret triggers as threats. And once the emotional response starts snowballing, it gets more difficult to handle triggers with curiosity or compassion.

Triggers emotionally hijack us, taking away our ability to reframe the situation. This is also called the *amygdala hijack*. Reactions to emotional stressors disable the higher cortex of the brain, preventing us from making a sound, rational decision. An emotionally hijacked person may become extremely reactive, defensive, and lash out at the stressor. When your amygdala 'hijacks' your brain, you may say things you later regret—send off an angry email; scream at your partner, colleague, or child; drink too much; or behave in other impulsive, destructive ways. It makes us go into this auto-response of being angry or defensive, and we find it difficult to change our response into a positive one.

We need to understand that by reacting negatively, we are causing damage to ourselves. You are either keeping this emotion unexpressed, causing illness, or transferring it to someone else, triggering a negative chain reaction. There is no upside to this!

Every action adds to your happiness. If you aren't happy in the day-to-day, you can't be happy over the long term. If you deconstruct a happy life, it comes back to the micro-decisions that you make when triggered. You need to learn to work with yourself and understand that constructing a happy life is based on changing your response. That is the building block of happiness.

Remember, happiness is cumulative. Every reframed response takes you closer to happiness.

Reframing your response

To be happy and successful in work, life, or love, you need to know how to get back on track when your amygdala hijacks your brain chemicals. How you channelize that trigger-generated emotion into the next positive step is key. At the point of the trigger, you need to be able to pause and reframe the response, give it a different meaning, and not go into a destructive deduction of the scenario as it presented itself.

In the above example, you could have saved the day by reframing your response:

- When you were cut off in traffic, your first impulse may have been to yell at the person. But, if you pause and think, you'll realize that the angry response isn't benefiting you. Instead of reacting with anger, you could have paused and chosen to interpret the situation differently. For instance, if you choose to interpret that the person who cut you off was rushing to a hospital, suddenly everything remains the same, but your reaction changes. A LOT. Then, you don't get angry at them. Instead, you feel sympathetic and you're willing to let it go…

compassion creeps in. Then suddenly you aren't yelling anymore, you aren't stressed about it.

- When you were interrupted in the meeting, you could have taken a deep breath, analysed your emotion at the moment and given the aggressor a measured response.

But reframing this response takes practice. To achieve emotional mastery, we need to understand that triggers and stressful situations will always be there, but it is our choice that causes the next action. You have the choice to not generate extreme emotion and take destructive action. The more we allow ourselves to get hijacked into a negative reaction, the further we stray away from happiness. If you allow yourself to be hijacked, then you're no longer in control. The less control you have over your reactions, the more damage you are going to cause to everything that is around you. You need to break the pattern!

To overcome the amygdala hijack, we need to reactivate the prefrontal cortex—the seat of our thinking, the brain's executive centre. Here is how you can do that:

Acknowledge the trigger → Pause → Check the hijack → Take action → Break the chain of negativity.

Awareness and acknowledgement are critical aspects of this process. Becoming aware that you are emotionally triggered, allows you to notice that your actions are under the influence of that emotion and, perhaps, you should wait to act till you can return to a level of stability.

The pause is equally important. It allows you to calm down—maybe drink a glass of water, take deep breaths, listen to music, or do whatever that helps you centre yourself. Learn to slow down and breathe before responding to the stressor so that the prefrontal cortex has time to get on board.

Learn to stay mindful of the hijack—deliberately redirect your mind from automatic worries and fears. Each and every time you face a trigger, take a pause and think, 'Hmm… What's happening here? I feel the anger bubbling inside of me. I'm tempted to say something mean. Would that be a helpful thing to do right now?' When you reflect on each and every emotional response, you will be able to see a pattern of your triggers and your responses. Gradually, this helps you recognize your triggers faster, resulting in a more thoughtful response.

You could also broaden your view about the person, the situation, or your own emotion. For example, if your manager gives you negative feedback and you feel triggered by it, you could broaden your view about the person by understanding that they have good intentions behind the feedback and would like to help you do better. Or, you could approach the situation differently, say, by considering that the appraisal process is designed to help improve your performance. You could also broaden your view about your emotion—you don't have to be triggered; instead, you could take this feedback and work on it.

Six methods to manage your emotional health

Emotional mastery is not just understanding your emotions and managing your responses. It also needs you to manage your overall emotional health. Here are six ways to improve your emotional wellbeing.

1. **Gratitude and kindness**

   Kindness is a behavioural response of empathy and compassion with actions that are selfless. This can lead to a sense of interconnectedness with others. When you focus on others, you are able to see things from their perspective and not react negatively even when triggers show up. If you are in a state of gratitude and kindness, your ability to forgive somebody in the moment is higher.

   This is the story of a man and a woman struggling to save their lives. The story plays out at the edge of a cliff where a woman is dangling, holding on to the man's hand for dear life. She can't climb up because a poisonous snake is peering out of the rocks. While the man's body, waist and below, is caught under a large boulder that's crushing him.

   The man thinks to himself, 'Why can't she try and climb a little harder? Can't she see that I'm in so much pain? Yet, I am still pulling her as much as I can.'

   The woman thinks, 'Why can't he make more of an effort to support me? The snake is going to bite me.'

The lesson here is that one can never know all the pressure the other person is under, and the other person often can't see the pain you're in. Life would be much better if we all made a little more effort in trying to understand each other.

Next time you get triggered, try to see the situation from the other person's point of view. Put yourself in their shoes. Learn to think differently. Be more open to different perspectives and opinions. A little kindness and patience can go a long way. Everyone we meet is fighting their own battle. If you wish other people to be more understanding, compassionate, and helpful to you, be all those things for other people.

2. **Exercise and meditation**

When strong emotions arise, a few deep breaths can often help you feel calmer. Yes, it's that simple. Mindful meditation practice can help you pay attention to your body and alert you when your emotions are taking over. Brain studies show that more mindful people have better communication between the amygdala and prefrontal cortex when reacting to an emotional stressor. Mindfulness works best when you have learned the skill by meditating regularly and practised it when you are not stressed. The key is to continuously reflect on becoming aware of your triggers before they hijack you emotionally. The more you reflect and deconstruct your emotions, the sooner you catch yourself getting triggered and respond mindfully.

In addition, exercise and other forms of active movement release the feel-good chemicals in the brain, helping you relax and override the emotional trigger. That's why a long walk is so relaxing!

3. **Self-compassion**

Learn to let go and be open and accepting of what is going on around you. Don't forget to be gentle with yourself and to avoid excessive self-criticism. Journaling and reflection will help you appreciate the goodness that surrounds you.

4. **Connect with others**

Don't bottle it up. Spend time with friends and family. Establish a strong support system. Be authentic and share what's going on— the good, the bad, and the ugly. Don't just vent. Be a good listener, too. Invite others to share and learn from their perspectives.

5. **Sleep and nutrition**

Quality sleep and a balanced diet can go a long way in helping you manage your emotional health. They help you stay in top form and at the peak of health, avoiding additional stressors caused by an unhealthy body and mind.

6. **Find a release**

Even with good emotional-health practices, there will be times when your emotions take control. One of the ways to deal with them is to find a safe release that works for you. For instance, writing down what's bothering me works brilliantly for me. Writing is cathartic for many people who use it as a way to release anger, frustration, sadness, and grief. Finding an empty place and screaming your lungs out also works. Punching some pillows and cushions might help, too. In fact, in Japan, a few companies have an 'anger-release room' where you can pin a picture of your boss and punch away!

Emotional mastery takes time and practice. It's like a muscle you have to build—it takes time and effort, but you can't give up. I have fallen off the track so many times, and still stumble at times; but there has been consistent improvement—and that is what's important. When you keep at it, you notice a gradual shift in your awareness, you start noticing changes in your response, you are calmer, more composed, and things start looking up for you. Your worldview has shifted—not because the world changed, but because YOU have changed.

When you work on your emotional responses and emotional health over a period of time, you will be able to develop a sense of control. You will be able to identify aspects that are within your control and do something about them. You will also be able to accept and make space for aspects that are beyond your control.

Karma in the mix

But, what if no matter how hard you try, the triggers just keep cropping up? What if, no matter how much you pause and assess and analyse, you keep reacting to these triggers the same way? This is your karma at play, and what you need here is healing. We'll talk more about that in-depth later in the book, but for now, understand this: every action you take adds to your karma, which is stored as karmic memory in your energy sheaths. This energy signature plays a crucial role in how you interpret a trigger based on your past trauma and respond to it.

Your karmic record is always directing you to certain actions to balance what you are carrying forward. So, in a way, your decisions and actions are influenced by this memory that you carry forward from different lifetimes—largely because it is seeking to get you to pay off the things that are pending and accept those where people have to give you in return.

Unless you clear this karma—unless you heal it—you will not be able to reframe your responses.

This is especially true of addictions. Addictions happen because there is a strong impulsive encoding within your system that doesn't allow you to respond positively to a trigger. Chainsmokers go for a smoke when faced with even the tiniest of conflict or stress. Emotional eating—we've all heard of it—is a form of addiction as well, where we turn to food to deal with triggers. These also manifest as substance abuse, compulsive behaviour, and other actions you do when you are hijacked, and your animal instinct takes over.

To overcome these karmic encodings, we need to be aware of these tendencies and focus on healing them. When you build an awareness of your triggers and an ability to be present, to be aware of your tendencies, and act in spite of the compulsive nature, you have achieved emotional mastery.

Your emotional mastery toolkit

Building your emotional muscle requires daily practice. Here are some tools and tips that can help you incorporate emotional fitness activities into your daily routine.

To deal with constant worrying

1. The Worry Tree technique

   • Notice the worry.

   • Ask yourself, 'What am I worrying about?'

- Ask, 'Is this a hypothetical situation or a current problem?' and/or 'Can I do something about this?'

- If the worry is a hypothetical situation: Let the worry go or postpone your worry until later. Change your focus of attention to the present moment

- If the worry is a current problem: Make an action plan. What to do, when to do it, how to do it, schedule it.

- Let the worry go in the meantime. Change your focus of attention to the present moment.

2. The Worry Jar technique

- Write your worries down on tiny slips of paper and put them into a jar or container to get rid of these thoughts for that moment.

- Come back whenever you have the energy and time to think about it—set aside a fixed time to think about these issues, say 5.00 p.m. to 6.00 p.m.

- Go through your worries again. Think about whether it's still something you worry about. If not, you can rip them up and throw them away.

- If it's still bothering you, think about what you can do about it—find a solution. Most importantly, accept these thoughts and take full accountability to find a solution without blaming external situations or people

* Notice the Worry

* Ask yourself "What am I worrying about?"

* Ask: "Is this a hypothetical situation or a current problem?"

and/or "Can I do something about this?"

* If the worry is a hypothetical situation - let the worry go or postpone your worry until later - change your focus of attention to the present moment

* If the worry is a current problem - make an action plan: What to do, When to do it, How to do it, Schedule it

* Let the worry go, in the meantime - change your focus of attention to the present moment

THE WORRY TREE TECHNIQUE

To prevent overthinking

- Notice the quality of your thoughts.

- If you see yourself worrying about something, take a step back and assess the odds.

- Reframe and replace your thoughts. The best way to do this is journaling; it allows you to introspect and assess the rationality of these thoughts.

To deal with grief

- Give yourself time to grieve and cry—vent your feelings. Holding onto these emotions without an outlet may disrupt your physical and mental health in the long run.

- If you didn't get a chance to say goodbye, write a letter to the person you have lost. Say everything you want to say—feel yourself become calmer.

To detox from negative news

- Do not constantly listen to the news.

- Schedule some time in a day, or occasionally, to read important highlights.

- Bank on other methods of recreation—spend time with family, read your favourite book.

REFLECTION TIME

DISCOVER

Download the *'Emotion Chart'* from your online Happiness Habits bundle. Keep it handy, and when you feel triggered, name the emotion, and call it out to yourself.

Learn how to release an emotion

Ask, *'Where in my body do I feel this emotion?'*

Label it: Give it a colour, picture its shape, see if it is moving?

Feel it completely, experience it, and then ask, *'What message does it have for me?'*

If there is a message, ask yourself, *'What can I do with it?'*

After acting on the message, ask, *'How do I feel now?'*

If you are disturbed, slow down your breathing. Try to get your number of breaths to seven or less per minute. As you do this, imagine the emotions that distress you leaving your body.

Understand how emotions show up in your body

Choose emotions that you want to feel in your body, such as happiness.

'Where am I feeling this emotion?'

'How do I know it?'

'What picture comes to my mind?'

'What is the sensation of this feeling?'

When you want to create this emotion in the future, think about these elements and use them to shift your emotions quickly.

DECIDE

Keep a log of your triggers. Use the tracker below to identify your triggers. Now, against each trigger point, note down your immediate response to the trigger, such as *'how did it make me feel?'* and *'how did it make me react?'* In the third column, note down, *'What would I prefer my new response to be?'*

TRIGGER EVENT	CURRENT RESPONSE	PREFERRED RESPONSE

STRATEGIZE

Create your own personal emotional-fitness action plan

Similar to a first-aid kit, create a list of three actions (to begin with) that you will do, should you find yourself worrying or being anxious. These could include anything from breathing exercises to mindfulness, or some physical activities, like going for a run. Focus on your *circle of control*—a set of things you can control. For example:

1. Eat healthily

2. Limit news and/or social media

3. Indulge in breathing and physical exercises

4. Do mindfulness exercises

5. Create healthy boundaries for yourself

6. Practise gratitude and positive thinking

7. Help others in need

My personal emotional-fitness action plan
1.
2.
3.

Living with Flow

'The best moments in our lives are not the passive, receptive, relaxing times… the best moments usually occur if a person's body or mind is stretched to its limits in a voluntary effort to accomplish something difficult and worthwhile.'

– Mihaly Csikszentmihalyi

Have you ever found yourself doing something that totally absorbed your attention? You were so engrossed, 'in the zone,' that you forgot how much time passed. You didn't even feel the hunger pangs or the usually compulsive need to check your phone!

That, my friend, is the state of *flow*!

Flow is when your body and mind are in sync. This seamless sense of fluidity between your physical self and mental state elevates you to a place where you are totally absorbed by and deeply focused on the task at hand. You feel like your senses are heightened. You are so engrossed that you lose track of time. You feel you are at one with the task at hand and create an effortless momentum to achieve more.

You can find a state of *flow* while doing something creative, you can find it while engaged in physical activity, and you can even find it in your day-to-day tasks. And when you do, according to psychologists, 'it will leave you feeling ecstatic, motivated, and fulfilled.'

As human beings, we are driven by our senses. In the pursuit of happiness, they play a major role in our self-discovery. Our sense of self is connected to our sense of accomplishment, which is one of the major drivers of our happiness.

In short, if you accomplish more, you feel happier. But how does one do that? We all have just 24 hours in a day, right? This is where *flow* comes in. By consciously creating a *flow* state, you can effectively and efficiently maximise what you do in a specific amount of time.

So, how do you go about creating this state?

There are two key components of living with *flow*—energy and focus. When you manage energy and focus—and both are interlinked in some ways—you gain the ability to be in *flow* for longer periods of time. Let's see how you can work with them to start living with *flow*.

Energy effectiveness

If I were to ask you to do an important task after you have been working hard all day, would you be able to give it your best?

Would you be able to be patient with your children and give them the love and attention they need if you have been sleep-deprived?

Would you be able to focus and perform your best in an important interview after a big lunch?

No, because you'll be fatigued and lethargic. You'll feel like you have no energy to do these things.

'Pretty much how you were earlier,' Neuro added, (not so) helpfully.

'Yes, and I know better now,' I grumbled.

You require energy for everything you do—physically, emotionally, and intellectually. You need energy to sustain your relationships, you need it to do your job better, you need it for physical activities like working out at the gym, you need it to be able to focus on important things.

To be able to do anything effectively, you need to manage your energy cycle. Yes, all that juggling you did to manage your time better could have given better results if you managed your energy instead!

How do you do that? Well, by understanding what drains your energy versus what gives you a boost of energy. It's instinct as much as science.

No one can be at peak energy at all times. Throughout the day, you will have cycles—called ultradian rhythms—of high and low energy, based on what's termed as your chronotype.

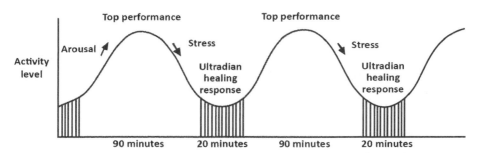

Adapted from: Rossi, EL: The 20 Minute Break, Tarcher Putnam, New York, 1991 p. 12

An important thing to note here is that all of us have two or three periods of peak energy, which typically last for about 90 minutes each. When you are in tune with your senses, you can recognise these periods of natural high. Now the smart thing to do is to use these peak energy periods to get in a state of *flow*.

Energy effectiveness is about understanding one's energy level and matching your energy with the complexity of the task at hand. Energy management can help you accomplish more in the same amount of time without making you feel overwhelmed or burnt out.

Sleep deprivation, caffeine dependence, an unhealthy diet, and a sedentary lifestyle can deplete your energy. Three critical components—sleep; morning routine that includes hydration, movement, and meditation; and nutrition—affect your energy levels and determine whether you can achieve the *flow* state or not.

Another major factor that influences your energy is your emotions. When you are not in tune with your emotions, you're unlikely to be in *flow* because your energies are all over the place, and your ability to focus goes away. This is why emotional mastery gives you the opportunity to be in *flow*. Positive emotions give you an energy boost, while negative emotions deplete your energy. A good way to get an energy high is to do more of what generates positive emotions for you.

Let's look at how small changes in your sleep patterns, morning routines, and nutrition can give you a major energy boost.

The power of a good night's rest

Do you wake up a lot during the night?

Do you feel groggy and tired when you wake up?

Do you feel sleepy throughout the day?

Do you need the help of caffeinated drinks before noon to keep you awake?

Then, my friend, you aren't getting enough sleep!

Sleep recharges your body and mind, and 7–9 hours of sleep is essential for adults to function at their peak capabilities. But most people consider sleeping for 7–9 hours as a 'waste' of time. They pride themselves on working with just 4 hours of sleep or pulling all-nighters. What they are doing is damaging their performance, throwing off their reaction time and judgement, and getting on a fast-track to burnout.

Nothing in this universe is wasted. Sleep takes up one-third of a human being's life—and much more than that for almost every other species in the world—for a reason.

You sleep because your body and mind need this time to rest, recuperate, and recharge. Sleep enhances memory, boosts the immune system, prevents disease, regulates metabolism, improves athletic performance, inspires creativity, and wards off mental illness. Not just that, your brain works to find solutions to problems while you are sleeping. I'm sure you have heard of people saying, 'sleep over your problems'—there is actually science behind this!

You can even leverage your sleep state to manifest the desired outcomes. Sleep essentially bridges your consciousness with your subconscious. As you near sleep, your ability to prime your subconscious is higher. In this state, one can use affirmation or an intention, or even a short meditation to help you, say, inculcate a habit. Or get you to quit something that you have been trying to quit.

When you sleep, you go through four stages of sleep that repeat cyclically through the night—every 90–120 minutes[18].

---

18. https://www.sleepfoundation.org/how-sleep-works/why-do-we-need-sleep

The first two stages are when you are in the process of falling asleep. These are stages of light sleep.

The third stage of sleep is the deepest sleep when healing and regeneration happens. The body focuses on cellular repair, muscle regeneration, and even immunity building. Your body is dealing with pain and fatigue and taking care of itself—you need to give it time to do so.

In the fourth stage, we dream. A big part of dreaming is about memory reconciliation and the healing of trauma. Your brain does these things by trying to let go of things, consolidating between your short-term memory and long-term memory, and releasing certain feelings or emotions that require sorting out. The dream cycle, therefore, is important in your memory processes.

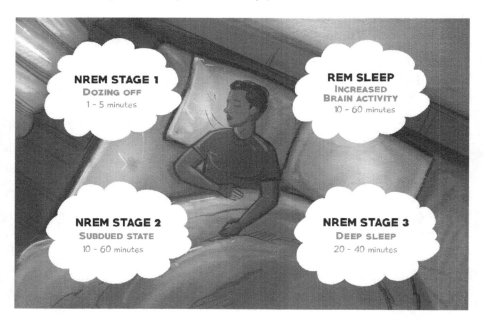

I have sleep apnoea, and for the longest time, I didn't do anything about it. Until I realized that it was affecting my performance. I loved quizzing and at just 26 years of age, I started forgetting stuff. I had access to so much trivia, but I couldn't recall it. Finally, a sleep specialist helped me figure it out. The sleep apnoea wasn't letting me get to the dream state. I kept waking up! And so, my memory wasn't getting consolidated and that led to me forgetting stuff. I finally started using a sleep machine to leverage the dream stage more effectively.

Even without a condition, most of us end up ruining our sleep cycles—often, unknowingly. We eat late meals, fiddle with our phones, go to bed at odd times, and do a number of things that interfere with a good night's rest. Even the environment that you sleep in—your bed, pillows, curtains, ventilation, etc., affect the quality of your sleep.

One of the biggest hindrances to sleep is the light in the blue spectrum. These 'cooler' shades of light are interpreted as sunlight by our body, and mess with the natural biochemical schedule of the body. The best way to get sound sleep is to sleep in complete darkness. If you are a late riser, invest in some dark curtains that keep the sun out. If you do need some light to sleep in, use 'warmer' shades in the red spectrum.

Twenty things that can help you sleep better to put your best foot forward in everything you do!

(Psst… you can download this checklist from your Happiness Habits bundle online)

1. Have your last meal at least three hours before your bedtime to make sure you process the sugar your body produces before you go to sleep.

2. Keep a regular sleep schedule. Once the body recognises and gets into a rhythm, it helps the body plan in releasing certain chemicals such as melatonin that help the sleep cycle.

3. Keep your phone and other gadgets away for the night. The blue light and the constant notifications make it difficult for you to get to sleep and fall into a deep sleep.

4. Have your last caffeinated drink at least six hours before your bedtime. Caffeine stays in your system for much longer and having it closer to bedtime will keep you awake.

5. Work out in the first half of your day or at least five hours before you sleep.

6. Read a book before you sleep; preferably a hard copy or on an e-reader with minimal blue-light emission.

7. Spend quality time with family or friends.

8. Journal your thoughts—what went well, gratitude, affirmations, etc.

9. Park at least 15 minutes for reflection before you sleep.

10. Use mindfulness techniques and meditation to relax your mind and get rid of the day's worries and anxieties.

11. Keep your room in complete darkness while you sleep, even after sunrise.

12. Ensure a noise-free bedroom or use calming sounds such as flowing water, sleep music, white noise, etc.

13. Use warm lights instead of blue and white lights as you wind down for the night.

14. Lie on comfortable and clean bedding, which is changed at least twice a week.

15. Keep your room at an ambient temperature of 24 degrees Celsius.

16. Let fresh air and sunlight in the room during the day while you are awake.

17. Keep the room smelling pleasant with fresh, light smells (for many, lavender aids in sleep).

18. Sleep in comfortable, soft, and fresh clothes.

19. Keep the bedroom clean, fresh, and clutter-free.

20. Take steps to ensure you don't wake up with a jolt.

How you wake up is as important as how you sleep. Alarming your body with a sudden sound puts it in a place of shock, and it does not give your brain ample time to organise a shift to a conscious state of mind. Keep your alarm away from where you sleep. It forces you to get up to turn it off, giving your body the signal to initiate a wake-up schedule by letting your conscious mind kick in.

When you wake up well-rested, you are recharged to tackle the day and everything that comes your way. The next step is to amp-up this energy with a morning routine.

Amp up your energy with a morning routine

A morning routine is not just for the early birds. You don't have to be up at 6.00 a.m. to follow it. A morning routine is just the first few things you do when you wake up. For most people, it goes something like this:

- Snooze your alarm thrice

- Wake up with a groan

- Check notifications on your phone and even respond to some

- Have something caffeinated as you get ready to go to work

And just like that, you've wasted all the good energy you woke up with.

Did you know you could make your entire day feel better just by tweaking a few things that you do first thing in the morning?

For instance, instead of first checking your phone with half-closed eyes, set your intention for the day. Visualize how you want the day to go. Then get up and drink a glass of water before anything else—preferably within the first 20 minutes of waking up. The body needs hydration, and you haven't had any water in the last 7–8 hours you've been asleep. Then, give yourself a few minutes to meditate or connect with nature. Get some fresh air, look at some greenery, sit with your journal and jot down some thoughts and affirmations. Breathe!

Do some quick exercises—even 10–15 minutes are enough. You don't need an elaborate routine; you can even do just jumping jacks or skip rope. When you exercise, the idea is to do that till you start breaking a sweat—that's the point your body releases chemicals that make you feel good—endorphins. If you work out in the morning, these feel-good chemicals last you all day long!

And finally, eat a healthy breakfast (yes, even you, intermittent fasters!) to fuel yourself up for the day.

20 minutes in the morning that will set you up for success all day long!

- Drink water
- Meditate, connect with nature, journal positive thoughts and affirmations (10 min)
- Do some simple exercises till you break a sweat (10 min)

Eat right to stay alert and active

'Why are we even talking about food? What's food got to do with happiness?' Neuro's voice echoed in my head.

'Well, the type and quantity of food you eat, and when you eat it, is very important to your wellbeing and your ability to accomplish things. And we've already established how wellbeing and happiness are linked together,' I responded to the voice of reason in its own language.

Food is fuel for the engine that is your body, and it won't be able to function on an empty tank. At the same time, if you fill up too much, you'll be sluggish and have low-energy levels as your body tries to digest the meal. This is typically why you feel sleepy after a big meal. All the blood flow is directed to your stomach instead of your brain! So, don't plan anything that requires a lot of brain power at least 30 to 45 minutes after lunch!

I'm sure you've heard that 'breakfast is the most important meal of the day'. Again, like water, your body hasn't had any nutrition in the 7–8 hours you have been asleep. So, you need to give it something to work with. But that doesn't mean you stuff it with carbs.

Carbs burn faster, and if you don't eat often, you'll feel an energy crash. Instead, eat lean protein or include foods with a low glycaemic index[19] in your diet that release energy slowly.

Avoid an energy crash at all costs because it overrides your system. When you are low on fuel, when you are hungry, making a conscious

---

19. A measure of how quickly a food causes our blood sugar levels to rise

choice to eat healthily and in moderation becomes close to impossible. You are now working under the compulsion to make some bad choices indeed! If this happens a lot, it could lead to food addiction. It's actually quite common! In fact, you may not even notice that you are addicted to caffeine or salty and sugary foods like chips and cold drinks.

Think about it. How many times do you rely on coffee to be alert?

Or are you one of those people who say, 'don't talk to me before I've had my cup of coffee.'

Coffee might feel like something that helps you stay awake, but all that is doing is blocking your natural indicators of tiredness and pain in the body. It's giving you an artificial spike of alertness. And so, when it wears off, you crash. Then you crave another dose of caffeine, and it becomes a vicious cycle—and just like that, you are addicted.

But keeping a few simple things in mind can help you eat healthier and stay hydrated.

- Hide the unhealthy food or make it inconvenient to get to. Studies have proven that people opt for what they can get to easily—the law of least effort. For example, put a bowl of salad right up front and hide the desserts somewhere behind other boxes.

- Eat on time. Pre-decide what you will eat at a time when you're not tired or hungry.

- Instead of trying to avoid unhealthy foods, focus on trying to eat more healthy foods.

- Always keep a water bottle in your line of sight.

Maximising your energy is a key ingredient in finding your happiness. It's the crux of everything you do in life. By understanding how energy works, and by applying it to get to a *flow* state, you can break free of the constraints of time, creating more meaningful outcomes and finding more value in life.

Focus for flow

While I contemplated living with *flow*, Sid popped into my thoughts again.

'Hey Sid, it's been a while,' I greeted him.

'Yes, and no,' he smiled. 'Yes, because I missed you and no, because you needed time to digest and act on my lessons.'

'There he goes on, in lecture mode,' I thought, only to be smirked at by the raven.

'You know I can hear your thoughts, right?' he said.

'Well, to what do I owe the pleasure of this visit?' I asked, trying to cover up my embarrassment.

'It's time to dig deeper and answer some questions,' he announced.

'Like a quiz? Is there a prize for winning?' I grinned at him.

'Does this look like a competition to you?' Sid rolled his eyes. 'The whole world is busy destroying itself with competitiveness and the need to show off. None of that nonsense here. This is about understanding, about wisdom,' he scoffed and changed the scene before my eyes. It was more like a slideshow, really!

First, there were tranquil rolling hills with a river gently flowing downhill—not gushing, not dwindling, simply moving.

Then, there were people skiing on snow-capped mountains, going down the slopes at a breakneck pace.

Soon, we were at the Olympics watching a pair of synchronized swimmers doing their routine.

From there, we went to a cricket match where a batter hit a six.

And finally, I saw myself playing snooker. I was pocketing the balls smoothly, feeling the perfect connection of my cue with the white ball. I could hear the perfect sound of the white ball hitting the red and the ball going right into the pocket. There, I felt like something was clicking into place. I wondered what life would be like if I could have this feeling every day!

Sid piped in, 'Do you know what was common in these scenes?'

'There was a certain grace to all of them,' I said. 'I could see that everyone was enjoying themselves and completely in the moment—just there and nowhere else.'

'Excellent,' Sid crowed. 'Now, tell me why? What is happening here? What is the reason for this grace, ease, AND fun?'

I closed my eyes and said the first thing that felt right, 'I think it's a convergence. Body, mind, and soul all coming together as one, with the entire focus on the moment and with no worries—just doing it to enjoy it with complete engagement in the activity.'

Sid was looking at me weirdly and then said, 'Wow! That was a great summary... but if I may, I have one small follow-up question. What do you think caused this complete engagement and presence? What clicked into place?'

I laughed, 'Sid, it may be a small question, but it's super difficult. Haven't I answered enough questions today? Why don't you tell me the answer to this one?'

'Fair enough,' Sid preened his feathers. 'The secret to living with *flow* is focus. You start by eliminating distractions and learn to single-mindedly focus on only one thing. Get your mind and body in a good space with the right energies, forget the past and the future, and just "be". Be fully present in the moment and completely enjoy what you are doing. Like when you are in love, time takes a different dimension. You have no sense that so much time has elapsed; it all seems like a minute. Your brain is on fire, and you have an abundance of energy. You have reined in your thoughts and aligned them in one direction. That, my friend, is *being in the flow*. And in this state, like the river that I showed you, life happens with grace, with ease, and even though there will be obstacles in your way, you have the awareness, the motivation, and the clarity to just move past that. Give your 100 percent to the current moment and you will transform the quality of your experiences. The more you can tune yourself to be in *flow*, the more meaningful your life becomes.'

'Wow! That was profound,' I exclaimed.

'That's not all,' Sid continued. 'The final question that remains is: Are you ready to do what it takes, to be like that river?'

'How do I know that?' I inquired.

'That, my friend, is for you to figure out,' Sid said, fading away and leaving me to my thoughts.

This conversation left me convinced that to express your best self, you also need focus. However, humans are wired to be distracted. And this distraction is again connected to our energy levels.

Have you ever daydreamed in the middle of something important?

Tried to focus on something but found yourself getting distracted with trivial things?

That's your brain, pulling you away from things that would expend more energy. The brain intrinsically wants to conserve and sustain energy levels within it, and if it finds the reserves low, it'll fight you when you try to focus. That's when your mind wanders, or you get that urge to check your phone or your social-media handles.

It's an impulse that's hard to control. When you see a snake, you don't stop and analyse whether it's venomous or not, right? Your first action is to put as much distance as you can between yourself and the snake. It's a survival instinct. Pretty much the same thing happens when your brain is low on fuel.

Moral of the story? If you want to stay focused, then make sure you manage your energy levels as we talked about earlier in this chapter. If you still find yourself getting distracted, then that's because your energy state and your schedule are not in alignment. And mostly, it's our habits and conditioning to blame.

For example, we live in a time that glorifies burnout.

'You did that, too,' Neuro was back, criticizing my life choices.

'But I don't do that now, right? Isn't that what matters... learning from your mistakes and moving on?' I shot back.

'Okay, okay, no need to go all "Sid" on me. One spirit guide is more than enough!'

The way things are, if you don't have puffy eyes from working overnight, or aren't constantly exhausted because of overworking, then probably you aren't doing enough, right? WRONG! If you force yourself to a high-pace state throughout the day instead of working according to your energy peaks and troughs, you are bound to crash sooner or later.

For most of us, the first peak of energy is after we wake up. You've got a good night's sleep, you've had a good breakfast, and drank plenty of water. Your systems are set to go! As the day progresses, these energy levels deplete. And that's fine. You may get one or two more peaks of energy depending on how you manage the day. These energy peaks are the times when you can focus best. To leverage *flow*, try to get more demanding things—tasks that require more focus, attention to detail, and thought—done in the first half of the day. Use the low-energy periods to do the routine operational tasks—approve things, clear emails, etc.

There is no set formula to manage your energy effectively. It varies from person to person. The idea is to get in tune with your energy and understand the signals your body and mind are sending you. To get more done in life, you need to tune your productivity to who you are. Instead of scheduling your day by time, schedule it by energy, and it'll make a tremendous difference to your quality of life.

Another deterrent to the state of *flow* is multitasking. **Multitasking is a myth**. Technically, you can say you do two things at once. For instance, you can drive a car and talk on the phone. You can clean and listen to music. But they are two entirely different things—a physical and a mental process. They use separate channels of your brain and body. And yet, your focus is compromised.

If you try to force multitasking, you are forcing your brain to make a quick context-switch, and that is immensely energy draining. If you keep doing it, you lose traction, you lose momentum, and you lose your ability to get things done properly. You end up breaking off one thing, revisiting it later and putting additional load on your brain to remember where you left off and access that memory once you are back. When you leave these open loops everywhere on a constant basis, it starts impacting your memory.

You cannot avoid multitasking altogether but try to keep it at bay as much as you can. You can do that specifically in your energy peaks with a few simple rules. For example, put your phone on silent, turn off all notifications, close all tabs that you don't need for your work, put up a do not disturb sign, etc. While at the office, you can put up a *flow card*

on your desk. Simply say, 'I am in *flow* and will be available after 2.30 p.m.' or any other message that works for you in keeping people from disturbing you.

To find yourself more and more in states of *flow*, it's important to replenish your energy throughout the day. Microbreaks work wonders for this. A really popular way to take microbreaks is the *Pomodoro* technique developed in the late 1980s by then-university student Francesco Cirillo. For myself, I use a 1,000-second timer (a little over 16 minutes) for my microbreaks. Every time it goes off, I take a one-minute break. I walk around, drink some water, and breathe… you get the idea. After 90 minutes, I take a 10-minute break. I use this to take a stroll, go talk to people, etc. What I avoid doing in microbreaks is checking social media. That's an attention sucker and can take your thoughts in a completely different trajectory.

While you can continue doing a task beyond your 1,000 seconds, without microbreaks, it burns up a lot more energy as you progress further without refuelling. Soon, you end up depleting it. And when you continuously deplete your energy without such breaks to refuel it, the energy expenditure is so high that by the end of your workday, you feel like you are spent. Soon, this consolidates and starts infringing on your quality of life.

At the end of the day, one of the major drivers of working is to provide yourself with a comfortable lifestyle. If you are depleted by the time you reach home, and you won't even have the energy to spend quality time with family and enjoy the things you love, then all of this would have been for nought.

5 things that will help you leverage *flow* better

1. Learn to manage your energy effectively

2. Align what you need to do with your energy cycles—keep focus oriented activities for peak energy time

3. Avoid multitasking

4. Take microbreaks to replenish your energy

5. Create an atmosphere that promotes *flow*: minimize distractions, play some background music, set up a timer

Have fun and live your life fully

Ultimately flow is about finding joy and happiness. Therefore, as you work towards it, don't forget that you will mostly find it in activities that you actually enjoy doing and have reasonable competency in. For example, if you know nothing about chess and you don't even like playing it, it's not very likely that you'll find *flow* in a game of chess. It's not possible to find *flow* in everything you do, but it's important to pepper your day with some activities that help you enjoy a state of *flow*. For instance, I love speaking to an audience and I can feel my energy pick up in sessions. I'm confident, energetic, and love every moment of public speaking. It leaves me with a feeling of accomplishment that, in some way, I did my best and made a difference to others. This feeling made me start my coaching sessions where I experience *flow*.

REFLECTION TIME

DISCOVER

Plot your energy levels throughout the day. Do it here or download the chart from your online Happiness Habits bundle.

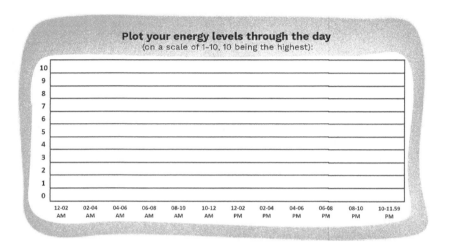

Here is the interpretation of your ENERGY PLOT:

Peak performance hours: Where your energy levels are 8 or above (typically we have 3–4 hrs of peak performance in a day)

Moderate energy hours: Where your energy levels are between 4 and 7

Dormant (sluggish) hours: Where your energy levels are less than 4

We are the most productive when we perform tasks according to our energy levels. To ensure the effective use of our time and energy,

- tasks which require **HIGH FOCUS** should be done in our **PEAK** performance hours

- tasks which require **MEDIUM FOCUS** should be done in our **MODERATE** energy hours

- tasks which require **LOW FOCUS** should be done in our **DORMANT** hours

Take a look at some of the activities that you do on a day-to-day basis at work and at home (please add any other activities in the space provided below):

Task/Activity	When do I typically do these activities? (If applicable)	What is the required focus level (high/ medium/ low) for this activity?	Is the task correctly mapped based on my energy level?	If not, can I change the time when this task/ activity has to be done?
Business-as-usual tasks (writing code, deskflow requests, etc.)				
Managing emails				
Attending team meetings				
Handling escalations				
Learning something new				
Client meetings				
Making Reports				
Brainstorming				
Household chores				
Browsing the internet				
Shopping				
Reading				
Preparing meals				
Watching shows/movies				

Task/Activity	When do I typically do these activities? (If applicable)	What is the required focus level (high/medium/low) for this activity?	Is the task correctly mapped based on my energy level?	If not, can I change the time when this task/activity has to be done?
Working out/sports				
Spending time with family (spouse, kids) and friends				
Recreational activities (watching sports, going for a movie, dinner, etc.)				

Take the '*Rate Your Sleep*' quiz in the Happiness Habits bundle.

Rate yourself on your morning routine:

Best practices for the morning routine	How do I fare?
First hour (morning stretches, hydration, making your bed, gratitude, meditation)	
Sustaining the morning groove (calming music, fresh air, intense exercise, affirmations, intent for the day, journal, reading)	
Morning must-haves (breakfast and visualization)	
Morning derailers (caffeine, checking work emails as soon as you wake up, scrolling through social media, rushing to work)	

What are some of the things that affect my state of flow?

Area of impact	What are the challenges I face here?
Energy management	
Nutrition and hydration	
Sleep	
Focus	

DECIDE

What do I need to do to find myself more and more in a state of flow? Identify some action items for each of the following:

Area of impact	What can I do to make it better?
Energy management	
Nutrition and Hydration	
Sleep	
Focus	

Would I like to change the time I go to sleep and/or wake up? _____

If yes, fill in the desired sleep and wake up time:

	Weekday	Weekend
Time I would like to go to sleep		
Time I would like to wake up		

Tick the sleep habits that you would like to adopt:

Checkbox	Sleep Habit	How will I incorporate these habit(s) into my routine?
	Having a consistent sleep and wake up time with at least 7.5 hours of uninterrupted sleep	
	Avoid snoozing the alarm clock	
	Switching off gadgets at least 30 minutes before I sleep	
	Having my last meal at least two hours before my bedtime	
	Avoiding the consumption of alcohol and smoking cigarettes	
	Having my last caffeinated drink at least six hours before my bedtime	
	Working out in the first half of your day or at least five hours before I sleep	
	Reading a book before I sleep (preferably a hard copy or on a device that does not emit blue light)	
	Spending quality time with family or friends	
	Parking at least 15 minutes for reflection before I sleep	
	Using mindfulness techniques and meditation to overcome worrying thoughts	

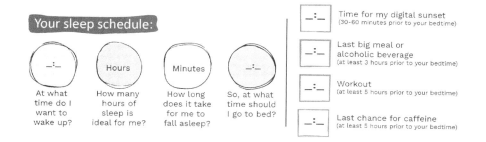

Your sleep schedule:

- **At what time do I want to wake up?**
- **How many hours of sleep is ideal for me? (Hours)**
- **How long does it take for me to fall asleep? (Minutes)**
- **So, at what time should I go to bed?**

Time for my digital sunset
(30-60 minutes prior to your bedtime)

Last big meal or alcoholic beverage
(at least 3 hours prior to your bedtime)

Workout
(at least 5 hours prior to your bedtime)

Last chance for caffeine
(at least 5 hours prior to your bedtime)

Tick all the elements that you would like to incorporate into your sleep environment:

Checkbox	Sleep Environment	How will I bring this change?
	Complete darkness while I sleep, even after sunrise	
	Noise-free bedroom or calming sounds (flowing water, Sleep music, white noise, etc.)	
	Warm lights instead of blue/white lights as I wind down for the night	
	Comfortable and clean bedding, which is changed at least twice a week	
	Ambient temperature of 24 degrees Celsius	
	Fresh air and sunlight during the day	
	Pleasant and fresh smells (like lavender, which helps in sleeping)	
	Comfortable, soft, and fresh clothes	
	Clean and fresh bedroom	

STRATEGIZE

What are the three things that I will include in my morning routine starting today?

Choose from the below or add your own.

	Spend at least 30 minutes to connect with nature (get fresh air and sunlight)
	Engage in 30 minutes or more of physical activity
	Spend at least 30 minutes every morning to learn something new
	Read a book for ___ minutes every morning
	Listen to calming music
	De-clutter my room (also ensure that the room is ventilated and gets sunlight)
	Eat a healthy and balanced breakfast
	Spend some quality time with family or friends

What are the three things I will stop doing?

Choose from the below or add your own.

	Snoozing my alarm clock
	Reaching for my phone to check messages as soon as I wake up
	Checking work emails, slack messages as soon as I wake up
	Going through my social media feed
	Reading the newspaper or watching/reading news on the phone/tablet within the first 30 minutes of waking up
	Having a caffeinated drink first thing in the morning (on an empty stomach)
	Wasting time in negative self-talk/complaining

What could be my potential derailers, and how will I overcome them?

_____

_____

_____

_____

_____

_____

_____

Healing

There was a time when I was dealing with a lot of health issues. This was right after I had that brush with death. And I had just started my healing process. But it felt like things were taking forever, and I needed some guidance. So, I did what anyone else would do in my situation— took a nap in hopes that my spirit guide would show up. He didn't disappoint, and this is how it went.

'Hey Sid, why do I have so many issues with my body? I've tried so many things to fix them, but I just can't seem to get rid of them,' I whined said.

Sid gave me a 'look' and said, 'healing isn't a race. It'll happen if it's meant to happen, and in its own time.'

'Wow,' I rolled my eyes, 'that helps a lot.'

I could see Sid struggling to not give me more snark, and finally he succeeded in containing it. After a long-suffering sigh, he said, 'You do know that your mind and body are connected, right?'

'Yes.'

'So, when there is a problem in your body, it means that, at some level, there is a play of the mind in there. For example, if you are operating from a place of fear in your thoughts and actions, then that insecurity gets reflected in your body as a big belly. The body accumulates fat as layers of protection and doesn't let go because it doesn't know what will happen in the future. So, if you want to lose that belly fat, beyond the diet and exercise, you also have to address that fear factor. If you don't address that, you'll keep coming back to that excess fat over and over again, no matter how many crazy diets you do,' Sid lectured.

'Okay, that makes sense,' I said. 'Let me paraphrase what you said to see if I really understood it. If I want to heal the various issues plaguing my body, I need to first figure out why that issue exists in the first place and what it is trying to tell me through the pain and discomfort. Right?'

'Spot on!' said Sid. 'And another thing, pain and discomfort also exist to help you take actions that will move you onto the trajectory that is more aligned with your life purpose. For example, once you identify the underlying cause—let's say it was fear—you take action to counter it. You may start a venture, take some risky decisions, act in spite of your fear—that action signals the mindset to change. You let go of the insecurity and, over time, the need for protecting yourself reduces and, gradually, the belly heals. So, you see, the pain led to transformation.'

'Simply put, to heal, I need to understand the pain, the insight it offers, and take positive actions to get relief,' I said. 'That's a complete reverse of what I do! Now I know why I am struggling so much!'

Healing is so much more than addressing just physical ailments

My troubles with sinusitis go back as far as I can remember. Every time I washed my hair, the next day I would be hit with an acute bout of sinusitis. I was almost constantly on medication, yet the issue would just not go away. When I started exploring healing modalities, a hypnotherapy session threw up something interesting. As a small child, I was caught peeping at someone washing their hair, a very innocent curiosity at my end that was nonetheless severely reprimanded. That incident left me with lasting guilt and shame that manifested as sinusitis. When I worked with a healer to let go of that shame, this decades-old ailment stopped affecting me the way it used to. This was such a drastic shift that my faith in some of these modalities went up manifold.

When you start working on the happiness quests, you'll often encounter blocks or resistance. And, sometimes, you'll just be stuck, or you might fall back into your old patterns. You'll see this happening over and over, in a loop. That's an indication that you need healing—to deal with past emotions, trauma, and negativity. None of the happiness quests are mutually exclusive, and healing has interlinkages with all of them. Healing is, perhaps, one of the most important aspects in our path to happiness. And largely not understood or not acted on.

When you heal, your pursuit of other quests becomes easier. You find everything becoming smoother and less challenging. This is because you shed a lot of the baggage you carry within you. This baggage comes in many forms—your beliefs, tendencies, compulsions, propensities—and is embedded in your psyche. It is a product of your past-life influences (karma) as well as childhood influences—especially the conditioning that happens till the time you are around eight years old.

These influences, in their worst form, manifest as compulsive behaviours and phobias. For instance, an unexplained phobia could be an imprint in your energy system that you have acquired at some point of time in your existence as a soul. For example, you may have a fear of water because, in some lifetime, you may have drowned. And, in this lifetime, when you see a water body, that past-life influence surfaces, and you feel fear for no apparent reason.

And it's not just fear. Even aspects such as judgment, lack of compassion, ego, and the need for control, hold you back on your quest for happiness. If you want to be truly happy, you need to evolve beyond them. And that's where healing helps immensely.

In our modern world, we want everything like our Maggie noodles, right? In two minutes, everything needs to get done. Often people say, 'I did this. It didn't work. So, this is all nonsense!'

Healing does not work that way. The intensity of what you have, what you need to learn, and where you need to go are all interlinked. And the progress is determined by how much work you're doing and what you need at that point in time. If you put in the work, something will shift.

The important thing is to be aware of this shift. These changes are so gradual that you don't notice, but they add up over time. The need for awareness is crucial because if you don't notice, your tendency to stop doing or giving it up midway is quite high. So, pay attention to the space you are working on healing and notice the difference.

For example, I have noticed that I now get less triggered in situations where I typically used to lose it! Another aspect that healing has helped me in is time management. I was late for everything! But as I started meditating, I bridged the gap. But it's not a one-time fix; I have to keep putting in the work to reap the benefits.

Ultimately, healing will alter how you think and feel, thereby getting you to make different decisions and take different actions. That is how the improvements happen, especially in places where people have been stuck.

The important thing to ask yourself is, 'What do I need to heal?'

The answer to that lies in the challenges that you face in your day-to-day life. Life is like a mirror. Anything that is happening in your life, good or bad, is a reflection of what is happening in your mind and body. Those are the keys that tell you what it is in your system that you need to really heal and learn more about. Your life reflects to you the opportunities to heal—be it your body, your emotions, your relationships, anything!

For example, in my own case, I had tried many things for years on weight-loss—diets, exercise, you name it! My regime was reasonably disciplined, but my results were not tallying with the effort. This is an indicator that, maybe, the issue runs deeper and that you need to look at healing as a modality. This does not mean I let go of my regimen; I just added healing to it. And in one of my hypnotherapy sessions, a memory of a past life when I was stabbed in the stomach surfaced. This was a trauma that was stored in my system and needed to be addressed before I could progress.

When you intellectually try certain things, and what you want to mitigate is not going away, that's normally a good indicator of where you need to look at it from a healing perspective.

This is the same for other issues as well. For instance, take a relationship. If something is not working, dive deeper to see what the challenge is trying to point you towards. Do you need to practise some level of forgiveness, compassion, or lack of judgment?

When you face a challenge in life, ask yourself, 'what is this challenge trying to point me towards? What do I need to really get better at?'

Healing encompasses all areas, but most times, we want to solve everything intellectually, in a scientific way that we are aware of. We try to treat symptoms and not the root cause. 'Oh, you have sinusitis, headache, IBS? Here, take this medicine...' But seldom do we stop and think, 'Why is it happening? What's the issue there?'

We don't ask these questions because some of these causes are encoded at an energy level—something that science has not been able to explain clearly. And this is where healing plays a major role. It is all about release. When you release that pent-up emotion that is stored in your system, things gradually improve.

For instance, before I tapped into healing, my life—my thought process and decision-making—was largely driven by fear. Fear of death, fear of the future, fear of failure, and so on. And it was holding me back from living my purpose. When I began my healing interventions, I realized that my fear is irrational in the larger scheme of things. I understood that my current life is not the end-all of everything. I understood that I am just a catalyst, here to do certain things. That I have a purpose and free will to act on it. But even if I don't end up doing everything I am meant to do, it's not a big deal.

We give so much importance to our current life, our family, our money, and our material belongings. We forget that, in the larger scheme of things, we are a minute speck in the great machine of creation. We forget that we have unlimited opportunities. This fear that you have, amounting to 'this is the only chance that I have', is overrated.

Healing through hypnotherapy, journaling, and breathing techniques helped me overcome my fears by giving me this larger perspective. It was exhilarating and freeing for me because I realized that the fear of death is not such a big deal.

Of course, at some point, this feeling from understanding may take a pause, and certain fears may resurface. That's when you realise that you've hit the limit of the understanding you gained from what you had worked on earlier. Now, you need to put in a bit more work. This realisation allows you more breathing space to make further progress.

Healing happens in layers. As you go through these cycles of healing, you go deeper and deeper into these practices. There is no particular end to this process. Like peeling an onion to reveal one layer after another, a new layer comes up every time. But every layer offers you some more learning and a slightly better sense of understanding of yourself. And you can sense this. It is not invisible.

Healing gives you the opportunity to pick what matters to you most and release that. By releasing it, you feel better, you know that it works, and it gives you the motivation to do certain things. And if you don't do it, you will be in pain.

This pain will come in the form of certain things not working again, giving you a clue that what you did might have been enough at an earlier level, but now you have to progress—like children progressing from kindergarten to primary.

So, now you do more work, then you release more, and then you go further. That's how the process of healing works.

A marker to indicate that you are healing is that the noise in your head reduces, and you become aware of your thoughts. You see things from a newer perspective of possibility. In fact, you start hearing a small, sane voice—the voice of your intuition that was smothered by the noise in your head. As the din reduces, this voice surfaces, and this is your true guide. For me, that voice was Sid.

So, the question arises, 'now, what can I do to heal?'

There are multiple options. At a higher level, some of the things that we are trying to heal are in terms of tendencies and influences, but also driven largely by our feelings of shame, guilt, fear, frustration, lack of acceptance, judgment, need for control, need for perfection, forgiveness, and lack of compassion.

Practically, if you ask, 'why do I have to heal?' You are trying to heal because you want to get beyond these things. This is because all these factors tend to hold you back.

'Then, how do I go about doing this?'

Since healing is a never-ending process, there are millions of modalities of healing. In this book, we'll look at the essentials of healing—practices that perhaps everyone needs to do every day. There are also alternative healing therapies, such as hypnotherapy, NLP, *reiki* energy healing, switch-words, *zibu* symbols, energy circles, crystals. You can choose what to go for depending on what your situation is and how comfortable you are with that modality.

Journaling · Meditation · Sound Healing · Yoga · Ho'oponopono · Mirrorwork · Breathwork · Chakra Healing · Cleansing your space · **HEALING MODALITIES** · Affirmations · EFT Tapping · Forgiveness · Blessing · Kindness & Compassion · Gratitude · Connecting to the elements · Grounding

Seventeen everyday healing modalities

For a guided experience of these modalities, you can access your Happiness Habits bundle on *www.happinesshabits.in*.

1. Breathwork

When you are exceptionally angry or frustrated, and you take a deep breath, have you noticed how you calm down immediately? Breath is life, and breathing is a healing tool available to you at all times. Here's how you can make breathing more effective:

- Incorporate breathing practices like *anulom-vilom*, *kapalbhati*, etc., in your morning routine for 10–15 minutes.

- Add visualization to your breathing. When you breathe out, visualize that you're releasing darkness, something that's holding you back—anger, fear, shame. When you breathe in, visualize a ray of white or pink light.

- Make time for deeper exercises like the *sudarshan kriya*.

2. Meditation

Meditation helps you rewire your thought process and improve focus. It helps you reduce negative thoughts and enhances your problem-solving ability. Here's a simple mindfulness meditation that you can do. You can follow a *'Guided Meditation'* available on your Happiness Habits bundle for your daily practice.

3. Yoga

Yoga, on its own, and with breathwork and presence, can counter many influences, and help in healing.

Let us take the extreme case of when someone requires healing, say, a person suffering from depression. When someone is depressed, they are caught in an inner negative spiral, and they're not able to find a way out of it. As long as they remain caught in it, they won't be able to see a way out.

There may be so many things that would be going well in their life, from an external point of view. Be it money, relationships, and so on. But they get caught in a spiral, and then they are not able to see a different point of view—they see life only through a certain lens.

When you do yoga with a certain presence, you are able to break out of those patterns—maybe momentarily, or maybe even for a longer period of time. But these practices afford you that opportunity to step out of your spiral through the practice by being involved in the practice.

4. Sound healing

Sound vibrations have a direct influence on our brain and, hence, have a direct correlation with our wellbeing and our thought process without us being aware of it. Unlike affirmations, sound transcends meaning. It's not processed by the intellectual mind but goes to the very core of our being. Ancient systems understood this power and all civilizations have chanting and songs as a part of their culture.

Certain types of sound produce certain waves in your brain, which are good for you. The more you expose yourself to some of these sounds, the more you give it the opportunity to impact you in a positive way. For sound healing, you can use tools like voice, drumming, tuning forks, and Himalayan singing bowls. So, put on that playlist with mantra chants when you start your day and see the difference!

5. Chakra healing

You have seven major chakras, with each of them having a role in your wellbeing. Your experience of life happens through these chakras and some of them, when they are blocked, tend to impact you.

For example, if I aspire to be a speaker and my throat chakra is blocked, then whenever I try to embark on my speaking journey, there will be certain hindrances.

Unblocking chakras with guided meditation, using light, sound, and colours, can increase your opportunities, intuition, and decision-making abilities. You can access a *'Chakra-guided Meditation'* in your Happiness Habits bundle online.

6. Journaling

An easy and powerful way to heal is journaling. It is, in fact, the simplicity of the practice that is the issue. Most people want complex things. It is difficult for them to acknowledge this. They say, 'how can I just write and get rid of it?' But that is the whole point of it—that you don't need external things. You can just use what you have.

Release journaling is about just that—release. Write about everything that's bothering you and you want to let go of, and burn the page, releasing that negative energy into nature. Set a time to do this on a daily basis.

7. Affirmations

Your thoughts and emotions affect your reality. Where you place your attention can attract the reality you desire. Affirmations are positive statements that can help you to challenge and overcome self-sabotaging and negative thoughts. However, you have to believe in these affirmations and feel them as the truth. When you say an affirmation, picture it as if it has already happened and feel the feeling it evokes in you.

Some examples of affirmations are:

- I am on the path to success
- I enjoy being fit and healthy
- I allow abundance to flow to me

8. EFT Tapping

EFT (emotional freedom technique) releases pent up emotions by tapping on certain 'energy points' in your body. You can access the *'Guide to Tapping Points'* in your Happiness Habits bundle online.

One of the good things about tapping is that you can work with it even for pain originating from emotional distress, like a headache from stress or a shoulder ache from dealing with a lot of responsibility. Assuming physical pain-causing reasons are taken care of, and yet, you are in pain—especially when it is recurring—then tapping works wonders.

9. Ho'oponopono

Ho'oponopono is a Hawaiian technique popularized by Dr Hew Len, which revolves around the four aspects of repentance, forgiveness, gratitude, and love. The Ho'oponopono prayer is simply repeating:

I'm sorry.

Please forgive me.

Thank you.

I love you.

These can be used in any sequence or order. I have used Ho'oponopono extensively to move forward in my happiness journey.

10. Grounding

Have you noticed the electrical grounding points in your appliances? All energy needs to be grounded. And what are we, if not energy systems? The charge within us needs to be grounded as well.

At a psychological level, grounding helps clear the noise in your head. When you are grounded, you're connecting at a deeper level, like growing a root into the earth. When you do that, your disturbances, anxiety, and fears dissolve to an extent. Of course, they don't go away completely, but, in that instance, you feel a sense of calm and clarity.

You can practise grounding anytime—first thing in the morning, whenever you're disturbed, or before an exam or an important meeting.

Here's how to do it. Stand in connection with the Earth. Imagine a white light going down your legs, growing roots into the ground, and reaching the centre of the Earth. And then imagine a gold or pink light coming back through the roots into your system and going up to your head. For other variants of this practice, check out *'Grounding Yourself'* guide in your Happiness Habits bundle online.

The effects of grounding are immediate and short-term. You can't think, 'I did the grounding exercise ten days ago. Why am I not feeling calm now?' However, practising it consistently will help you manage your stress and anxiety levels much better in the long term.

11. Mirror work

Motivational speaker Lisa Nicholas[20] has used mirror work to get out of tough situations. The practice involves standing in front of a mirror, looking into your eyes—ideally, your left eye, and saying affirmations or prayers or statements such as, 'I appreciate myself for *certain things*. I let go of *certain things*. I forgive myself for *certain things*. I commit to *certain things.'*

This approach bypasses your logical filters and affects your subconscious encoding. Of course, it needs repetition and regular practice.

Mirror work is more effective when you link it to other things in your everyday routine. For example, the best time for me to do mirror work is as soon as I come out of my bath, when I have ready access to a mirror. And I combine it with *Ho'oponopono*.

12. Gratitude

As soon as you wake up, smile, take a deep breath, think of all the good things in life you are grateful for, and set an intention for the day. Do this before you even get out of bed. Every day, find five new things to be grateful for, and do this for 21 days. Go beyond the big things and find small things to be grateful for.

Gratitude is so important that it is considered one of the fundamental shifters in healing. It changes the way you look at life and helps you refocus on the good.

---

20. https://www.motivatingthemasses.com/mirror-work/

13. Forgiveness

The lack of forgiveness creates toxicity in your system. If you are not able to release that, it festers. We often hold on to small insults so much that it affects the quality of our relationships. You end up focusing on the 10 percent that's going wrong and ignore the 90 percent that is good. Practising forgiveness will help you focus on the good—everyone has some good in them—and keep relationships positive.

A good way to do this is by practising radical forgiveness—a five-stage process that allows unconditional acceptance of what is, as is, because that's how it is meant to be. These stages include:

1. Telling the story: What happened?

2. Feel the feelings: How it made you feel?

3. Collapse the story: Withdraw the energy that you have given the story.

4. Reframe the story: Take a deep breath and reframe the story to see how that pain was necessary for you to learn.

5. Integrate: Let this possibility filter into your being and re-programme you from within to heal

Use the *Radical Forgiveness Worksheet* by Colin Tippings to help you through this process: *www.radicalforgiveness.com/wp-content/uploads/2016/05/Radical-Forgiveness-Worksheet-with-Radical-Acceptance-June-2016.pdf*

14. Kindness and compassion

Once, a little girl did not come home all day. Her parents frantically started looking for her. The police were called, the neighbours informed, and everyone was looking for her. A watchman at the mall nearby heard the commotion and asked what had happened. When he heard about the girl, he said she had to be somewhere in the mall. The police asked him, 'how can you be so sure she is in the mall?'

The watchman said, 'this girl comes to the mall often, and whenever she comes, she wishes me a good day both while coming and when going. She came in today and wished me once, but she hasn't wished me while going out. So, she must be still here.'

The police said, 'how can you remember one girl wishing you from so many people coming in the mall every day? You might have easily missed her.'

The watchman said, 'no, she is the only one who wishes me, and I can't forget her face.'

So, the police started looking for her inside the mall and finally found her locked out on the terrace.

One simple act of kindness from that girl left a big impression on the watchman, and that helped her in her time of need.

Sadly, in this world, our system is designed such that kindness and compassion are often considered as weaknesses. When a person is kind, they are misrepresented as 'a loser' and that they 'don't know how to be in the real world' or that they are 'not practical'.

This is far from the truth. Kindness and compassion require you to be a lot more in control. It centres on how you come across to others, and often, people don't want to make that effort. They say, 'I just want to be myself', and that's okay—as long as they're not offending somebody else.

Take, for example, the simple act of giving feedback. You can scream and shout at people and tell them that everything they did was wrong. Or, you could start with the good and then give constructive feedback on where they went wrong and how they can fix it. When you give feedback with the intent of saying it in a way that the person will be motivated to change, then it just clicks. Instead of that, if you just say what you think, people will get defensive. They won't understand where you're coming from. There is not enough empathy in that message.

When it comes to kindness and compassion, it is always about how you treat people. When you learn to be kind and forgiving, and compassionate, some people may change, some people may not. It is not about the result; you do it because that's who YOU are.

15. Blessing

Blessing is an extension of gratitude as it conveys and creates a positive connection with the energy systems of things. It's as simple as saying, 'I bless this water. I bless this food. I bless this…'

I recently read about a Japanese researcher who conducted a study on water, where he isolated some of it. He cursed one portion while blessing the other and took microscopic images at a molecular level. It is said that he observed a pleasant arrangement in the molecules that were blessed versus a very chaotic arrangement in the cursed ones[21].

Bless everything in your life—including the problems—and do it as a ritual. If you don't remember to bless everything, focus on blessing your water at least. Bless the water you drink and the water you bathe with. It'll cleanse your energy systems.

16. Cleanse your space

We talked about how important our space is for our energy, focus and general wellbeing. A stagnant environment is not conducive to happiness. Here are some simple things to cleanse your space:

- **Declutter**: Cluttered spaces accumulate negative energies and feel oppressive. Remove everything that is non-essential. Clean out your wardrobe, your table, your fridge—everything. Holding on to things is like holding on to the past. Only when you let go of the stale can freshness make its way in.

- **Use salt and incense**: Salt purifies and cleanses the environment of negative energies. Get a salt lamp and keep it burning in a corner to avoid clogged energies or add salt to your bathwater. Walk around the house with four to five incense sticks to cleanse the air.

- **Keep your space ventilated**: Better air circulation is directly proportional to a better thought process. Keep the windows open, air out your room, and even air your bedcovers and mattresses regularly.

17. Connect to the elements

We are made of elements. When you enhance the connection with these, it heals you and makes your soul happier. And it doesn't even take much effort! Here are a few simple things you can do to enhance this connection:

---

21. "The True Power of Water: Healing and Discovering Ourselves" by Masaru Emoto, Google Books

- **Sunbathing**: A great way to connect with nature and up your Vitamin-D levels. Just sit outside for half an hour between 10.00 a.m. and 11.00 a.m. and feel the energy!

- **Walking barefoot**: The feel of the earth on your feet is delightful. If it's on a patch of grass, even better! And as you walk, be mindful of your surroundings.

- **Take a salt-water bath**: Who doesn't like a soak in the hot tub? Just add salt to that and settle down to heal!

- **Get a massage**: Massaging unblocks the stuck energy in your body and helps unclog your energy systems, making you feel better instantly.

Put in the work

Most of the time, when people think about healing, they think of alternative therapies like *pranic* healing or *reiki*. While these practices do give you relief and help you get out of the negative spiral you are in, they are quick fixes. If you want to heal in the long run, you have to focus on the everyday practices and put in the work.

Healing is about addressing the issues encoded not just in your conscious memory but in your body and soul too. For healing to work, you need to change the entire system. Choosing to do some important practices, such as gratitude, journaling, and meditation, can bring in that shift and lead to a happier you.

REFLECTION TIME

DISCOVER

List down some challenges that you face in life.

What is it that never seems to go away no matter how hard I try?

_____

_____

_____

_____

DECIDE

Which of these healing practices would I like to include in my life? Pick at least one.

Healing Practice	Include (Y/N)
Breathwork	
Meditation	
Yoga	
Sound healing	
Chakra healing	
Journaling	
Affirmations	
EFT tapping	
Ho'oponopono	
Grounding	
Mirror work	
Gratitude	
Forgiveness	
Kindness and compassion	
Blessing	
Cleanse your space	
Connect to the elements	

STRATEGIZE

What are the specific things I plan to do for the healing practice I have chosen? How will I make it a habit that sticks?

_____

_____

_____

_____

Living Mindfully

Happiness is like a string of pearls—strung together to give you lasting happiness. Every pearl in that string is a moment where you are fully present and experiencing life or whatever it has to offer. For example, you are in a park and need to go from point A to point B, and you are walking there. Now there are two ways to do that. Either you just run across, disassociated with everything else along the way, or you walk mindfully, experiencing how the grass feels under your feet, how the breeze is cool on your skin, and how the flowers add colour and fragrance to their environment. In both cases, you get from point A to point B. But which way lifted your spirits and your senses? Which way made you calmer and perhaps put a smile on your face? Deep down, we all know the answer.

It's not that the walk will be smooth. You might step on a pebble and feel pain, but that pain will also heighten your consciousness of how much better the grass feels. Without pain, we cannot appreciate joy. Remember, nothing in this Universe is wasted. So, every step in your walk has a purpose.

All of us are on this journey from point A to point B—from birth to death. Everything in the middle are just moments to experience mindfully.

The biggest obstacle on your path to happiness is not external but internal, especially our 'monkey mind' that wanders. In fact, research shows that humans tend to be lost in our thoughts for 47%[22] of our day. Imagine, for almost half the duration of our day, we are following our monkey mind around! And because of that, we never fully enjoy anything.

---

22. Killingsworth, M. A., and D. T. Gilbert. 2010. "A Wandering Mind Is an Unhappy Mind." *Science* 330 (6006): 932–32. https://doi.org/10.1126/science.1192439.

Of course, not all the daydreaming and ruminating we do is a bad thing. In fact, it is a healthy and necessary process. It is only when we tend to get caught in these spirals of thoughts, following one worrying stream to another, and end up losing a chunk of our time, that we need to step in to bring our mind back.

The thing is; your mind is attuned to a negativity bias. We talked about it earlier—how this tendency to spiral into negative thoughts keeps you away from happiness. How can you focus on the good things when there is a constant script running in your head telling you all the ways everything can go wrong? The moment we transcend this involuntary background loop through a conscious and controlled approach, we successfully achieve a state of mindfulness. This is why practising mindfulness is so critical to happiness.

Mindfulness is a journey

A student seeking the mindful way of living, the Zen, asked his teacher, 'Master, if I work very hard and diligently, how long will it take for me to find Zen?'

The teacher thought about this and said, 'Ten years.'

The student thought that was a long time. He wanted it now! So, he asked, 'But what if I work very, very hard and really apply myself to learn fast, how long then?'

The teacher replied, 'Well, twenty years.'

'I don't understand,' said the disappointed student. 'How will it take me longer if I work harder?'

The teacher replied, 'When you have one eye on the goal, you only have one eye on the path.[23]'

Mindfulness is not a goal; it's a path that you choose to walk every moment of every day. It's a way of living that could totally change your life and make it happier and more fulfilling in all dimensions.

It took me a long time to understand that. There was a time when I put the demands of my work over everything else. I was so immersed in responding to what life threw at me, that I was never able to focus in the moment. I would constantly be checking my phone and my emails; I would be thinking about what I need to finish at work the next day or what my colleagues or boss said about something. It took away my ability to be present in other areas of my life, and they suffered.

For example, on weekdays after work, I had just a little time to spend with my kids before they went to bed. And earlier, while I would be physically present for them, my mind would wander—I'd be on my phone or think about something else. I felt that I was being a good parent by taking out this time, but was I really there? When I started down the happiness journey, I realized that I never really experienced those moments, and as a consequence, neither did my kids. So, I made a conscious decision to be present for them. And that completely changed our interactions! Now there is so much laughter, fun, and goofiness in that time, which was completely missing earlier. Just a small choice to focus my attention in the moment with my kids made that time so special for all of us.

And that's a connection most of us miss out on. We don't realize that by not being present in the moment, we are compromising our life

---

23. *The Haste: A Story About Mastering Zen* http://mindfulspring.com/mindfulness-and-zen-stories/

experiences. And we all do that. We are used to living on autopilot and taking things for granted.

Have you ever gobbled up a meal because you had to rush to something, and have forgotten what you ate?

Have you been in such a hurry that you forgot if you locked up behind you?

Have you been so lost in thought that you don't know which route you took to get to a place?

Have you been so busy taking pictures that you didn't actually see the sunset except from behind the lens?

These are signs that you're not experiencing life to the fullest. And what is happiness if not an experience! If you don't take time to appreciate the flavour of food, or the beauty of a route, or the stillness of a sunset, then *what* is the point of life?

When you don't pay attention to small moments, you lose the capacity to find joy in them. Then it takes a bigger thing to make you feel good. That's when people start seeking 'highs' and 'addictions' to make them feel good about life. On the other hand, if you start focusing on small moments, even mundane things become interesting experiences.

That said, mindfulness is not just about being present for the good things. It's about experiencing and paying attention to the present moment, non-judgmentally. So even if something is making you sad, or angry, or hurting you, pay attention to it. Dig deeper and find out why, so you can frame your response accordingly.

Living inside a time machine

For a moment, let us focus on what your negativity loop is really telling you. What do you tend to worry about incessantly? Usually, you'll find yourself thinking about something that went wrong, something that could have been handled differently, something that you cannot control but wish you could. You then take this a little further and start ruminating over what might happen as a result of this worry. What might be the reactions to your past response or lack of it? What other problems can this lead to?

Here you are, sitting in the present trying to enjoy a book, while your mind is focusing on the problems of the past, and the likely or unlikely problems of the future.

This toggling between past and future is a constant interference to us enjoying our present mindfully. In fact, if there was a system to download and analyse, say, 10,000 thoughts that your brain houses right now, a huge chunk of them would be either that of the past or those of the future.

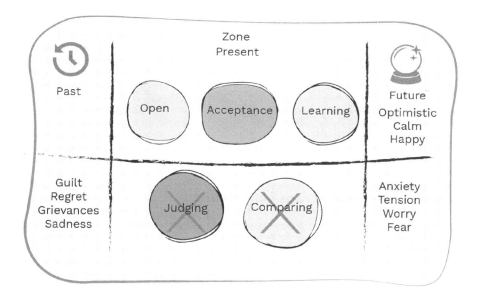

Let's assume that someone said something hurtful or nasty to you. At that moment, if you are fully present, your ability to respond is elevated as a whole. On the other hand, if your head is in the past, the same thing could trigger you, make you relive past trauma, feel that you have been insulted, and place you into a trail of emotions where you lose control of yourself and your present context.

To be more mindful, we have to train our thoughts to be in the present. The more you are in the present, the less time and mind-power you will dedicate to worry about your past actions or future projections. As you accumulate these pleasant moments of the present one by one, your day becomes better—soon, your week, your month, your year, and your life as a whole becomes happier.

Life will never be without its ups and downs. The key to happiness is in realizing that and ensuring with your thoughts, beliefs, values, and actions that you are able to *stay happy* in the downs.

A mindful life

How do you go about being mindful, then? There are five key areas that you need to work on:

1. Reduce the overwhelm caused by thoughts

2. Reduce distractions

3. Overcome emotional derailers

4. Practise being fully engaged

5. Practise being non-judgmental

Let's take a look at some of the tools and techniques that will help you do this.

Reduce the overwhelm caused by thoughts

The most effective way to deal with runaway thoughts is, of course, to regain control. You need to consciously pause, analyse, and call your mind back. Here are a few effective techniques you can start with in your everyday life each time you feel like your mind is overwhelmed with intrusive thoughts:

1. **Capture your thoughts**: Writing down our thoughts in a journal or using a digital journaling tool is a great way to understand what we are feeling and why we are so overwhelmed, as well as to take a pause and redirect our mind.

2. **Empty the mind**: Make a conscious effort to empty your mind of distracting thoughts to focus on the present moment. Thoughts and distractions build up over time, so you need to clean them from time to time. Only when you get rid of the old, can you make space for the new.

3. **Meditate**: Meditation rewires your entire system and reduces stress levels. However, like any new habit, it takes practice. There

are multiple apps and videos these days that help us take small steps towards meditation and calmness. Find your process, start small, and keep at it.

4. **Mindfulness cup**: This is an efficient technique to sort through your thoughts. Visualize a cup and fill it with everything that is going on in your head. That clears out the rest of the space for what you have to focus on now.

5. **Breathing exercises**: One quick and easy way to focus your mind back to the present is by focusing on your breathing. You can do breathwork meditation, *pranayama*, or just take steady deep breaths for a few minutes till you feel centred and grounded again, and you notice that the feeling of anxiety has passed.

Reduce distractions

The sheer volume of distractions that an urban working professional lives with is mind-boggling! Constant notifications from our various devices, hundreds of messages from various sources coming at us every hour, and even the expectations to multitask and hyper-task! It is no wonder that most of us are stressed, burnt out, and are unable to think straight!

The more external things you allow in your space, the more they hijack your thoughts. And these distractions pile up. If you keep adding junk to your brain, you'll have a constant tug-of-war when it comes to mindfulness. In a hyper-stimulated environment, our ability to enjoy something fully is compromised.

The most important aspect of enjoying our present to the fullest is to do away with all possible distractions. Checking every notification on our device, following a certain news 24X7, making sure there are no new work emails every few seconds—all of these have become major players in distracting us from our real-life experiences. The best way to manage this is, of course, to take stock of what distractions we really need in our life:

Do you really need all those pings and beeps from every single group on every single app you have on your smartphone?

Is each and every message you get a higher priority than you living your life?

Do you even want to be on that WhatsApp or Telegram group?

You know the answer to these questions already. Generously, mute groups and switch off all inessential notifications. Prioritise experiencing the present over that next meme.

Now that you have muted your notifications for a certain period, take stock. How many of those apps were, in fact, entirely unused? Are they essential to you at all? And if not, why even keep them around?

You can do this at work as well. How many browser tabs have you habitually kept open? After the notification management of these, there would definitely be a few that were entirely redundant. Close all such tabs to prevent them from distracting you from your most important task at hand.

Overcoming emotional derailers

A negative thought loop implies your mind is feeling negative emotions—fear, anger, worry, and anxiety. Something in our present triggered our past emotions, and now, we are stuck in this unpleasant headspace. How do we pull ourselves out of this? This is where emotional mastery that we discussed previously comes in.

To overcome emotional derailers:

- **Take stock of trigger points**: What sets you off most often? What was it about your past that triggered that angry reaction or brought on the panic?

- **Pause before responding**: Now that you have a stock of your trigger, you are a lot more conscious of your present than before. The next time you get triggered by an event, pause. You know this one. It is on your list.

- **Reflect on your response**: What would have been your usual response. What would you like it to be? When you are aware of your triggers, you are better equipped to analyse the situation objectively and to see other perspectives.

Practise being fully engaged

Staying deliberate with our physical senses is the steppingstone to staying deliberate with our thoughts. Practising the following simple elements is a great place towards our journey to mindfulness:

- **On waking up**: From opening your curtains to making your bed, keep your mind focused on everything you see and hear. How does the sunlight stream into your room? What are the first noises you hear? What is the pattern on your quilt? Notice. Ground yourself to what your senses are receiving from the get-go.

- **While eating**: Focus on what you are eating. What are the different textures? What are the flavours you are experiencing? Your sense of smell, sight…everything comes into play while eating. Focus on what each sense is absorbing.

- **While Driving**: Set yourself smaller targets while driving. For example, focus on how many times you honk. Try to cut down on unnecessary honking.

- **While walking**: Experience each step as your feet touch the ground. Feel the breeze. What are the sounds around you? What are the smells around you? Immerse yourself in the moment.

- **While listening to someone speak**: Make eye contact. Remind yourself to nod encouragingly, smile, and express accurately at the right times. Remind yourself that a good listener should ask engaging questions. All these will keep you focused on the conversation.

Practise being non-judgmental

A lot of unhappiness in life stems from our inability to accept things for what they are. And if you continue to fester those thoughts and feelings that stem from judgment, you'll be caught in a loop of anger, shame, and guilt. The SOLD technique can help you be non-judgmental and more accepting of everything around you.

Slow down the speed of your conclusions. Ask yourself – What are the possible causes of the situation or a person's behaviour	Observe the situation and state it the way you observe it. Use the phrase, 'I observe that…'	Look for possible alternative causes of behaviour – consider both internal and external causes	Disengage your assumptions, and also look for data that may be contrary to your observation

While practising being more accepting, also focus on gratitude and forgiveness that we talked about in the chapter on Healing. These practices help you focus on what's important and help you move forward on your journey to happiness.

When you start living mindfully, you'll realize that all those artificial stimulants were just giving you a momentary high. The REAL happiness is in slowing down and it comes down to how much you enjoy the little things. As they say, stop and smell the roses!

REFLECTION TIME

DISCOVER

Take the *'Are You Living Mindfully?'* quiz in the Happiness Habits bundle to find out how mindfully you live every day.

How do I think living mindfully will help me achieve happiness?

_____

_____

_____

_____

DECIDE

Write down a few things you will do in each of the below areas to live more mindfully.

Mindful Living	How will I do this?
Reduce the overwhelm caused by thoughts	
Reduce distractions	
Overcome emotional derailers	
Practise being fully engaged	
Practise being non-judgmental	

STRATEGIZE

What could be the potential derailers on this quest? How will I overcome them?

_____

_____

_____

_____

Living the Seven Quests

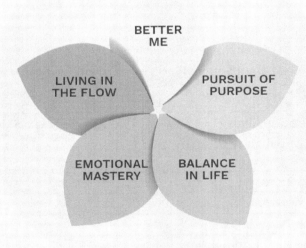

MINDFULNESS

HEALING

BETTER ME

LIVING IN THE FLOW

PURSUIT OF PURPOSE

EMOTIONAL MASTERY

BALANCE IN LIFE

When you remove a petal from a flower, while it may still smell sweet, there is a bit of it missing that doesn't allow it to be whole. It is the same for your happiness journey with the seven quests. While efforts in any dimension will improve the quality of your life, you must progress across all dimensions to experience happiness fully.

Depending on where you are in life, you start on different levels of the quests. Every dimension has levels of proficiency, and you must arrive at an equivalent stage across all seven quests to move to the next level of happiness. You can take assessments and figure out where you are in your journey and map your happiness quest on the online *7-Quest Experience* that is available on *https://happinesshabits.com*.

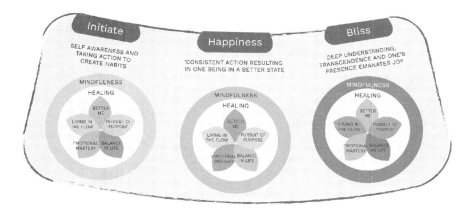

This framework is a good measure of identifying where you are stuck on your happiness quest. Usually, if you find yourself stuck, it would be because you are focusing too much on one dimension and ignoring the others. If you stagnate on one quest, it'll hold back your progress on others as well. As I mentioned at the beginning of this section, happiness is holistic and cannot be found in just one aspect of life or in external things. Happiness comes from this inner journey that transforms you—your thoughts, beliefs, values, and actions.

Upgrade Your Life

'Successful people are just those with successful habits.'

– Brian Tracy

Happy people are just those with happiness habits.

Make Happiness a Habit

You've made it this far and now you know what you need to do. The challenge is consistency, right? All these things look so simple. How difficult could it be to drink water in the morning or journal your thoughts? Yet, we keep failing to follow through on what we decide to do. And that's totally normal and expected. You are bringing in changes to your thoughts, beliefs, and actions. It can be simple, but it's not necessarily easy. And trust me, willpower is overrated. In fact, research shows that willpower runs out under stress. You can't rely on willpower alone to drive behaviour change; what you need is to train your subconscious mind with habits.

In short, you need to figure out how to make happiness a habit.

There are powerful resources out there on the science of habit creation, be it Charles Duhigg talking about *The Power of Habit* or James Clear showing us the magic of *Atomic Habits* or Nir Eyal explaining how we get *Hooked*. They all talk about the *habit loop*—how we get stuck in one endless loop of cues, routines, and rewards. You can access a toolkit to break out of bad habits or create good ones in your online Happiness Habits bundle.

When you decide to make changes in your life, it's exciting to try and do everything at once. But the secret to success is in starting small. This way, it does not feel like your entire life is changing overnight. You still get the comfort of familiarity. Once a new small habit is ingrained, you move on to the next and you keep adding it on.

When I started making changes to live a happier life, I chose 12 rituals across the seven quests to practise every day. Here's what they looked like:

Twelve rituals that make my day

1. **Shutdown challenge**: I eat my last meal for the day as early as I can—ideally, three hours before bedtime. From Sunday to Thursday, I avoid TV, laptop, and phone at night to improve my

quality of sleep. In addition, I changed my curtains to ensure my room is pitch dark at night to ensure deep sleep.

2. **Prime the subconscious challenge**: I create a pre-sleep routine. I review my day and look at what went well, ask myself what magic happened today, repeat a few key affirmations in my head or write them if I can, then say a quick thank you and ideally listen to a reprogramming audio and fall asleep.

3. **Super morning challenge**: I wake up with a smile, say what I am grateful for this day, take a few deep breaths, ground myself, and set an intention for my day. Then I drink water and clear my space by letting fresh air in, lighting a lamp, or using incense. I spend some time exercising, meditating, and visualising my ideal future and ideal day. I also practise breathwork and journaling to get messages, release emotions, practise forgiveness, etc.

4. **Bath routine**: I use salt in my bathwater with an intention to cleanse my physical and energetic body. I bless the water to take away impurities, leaving me in a positive frame of mind. I also take a mindful bath; I feel the water, smell the soap, and so on. I use this time to also thank my ancestors for their guidance and offer them some water. This is also my time for Ho'oponopono and mirror work. And every now and then, I leave a note for my wife expressing my appreciation for her.

5. **Kickstart work-day challenge**: The first thing I do is declutter my space and my mind. I put things on paper, prioritise the top three and do a quick energy mapping to schedule them—difficult things in a high-energy window and easy things during low-energy windows. I keep these must-do items in my line of sight, using a sticky note, a pad, or a board. I use a calendar and reminders to block time for planned important actions, play some inspiring music, and set up the right aroma using a reed diffuser. Before diving into work, I take seven deep breaths and set an intention for a great day.

6. **My during-the-day challenge**: I stick to my plan as far as possible and do the difficult things first. I do one thing at a time, and batch together the quick wins. I use high-energy windows for flow activities, take micro-breaks, and stretch from time to time. I play inspiring music in the background or on headphones.

I set micro-intentions for important outcomes, close all tabs when I am working, and write down important notes or to-dos.

7. **My mindfulness challenge**: I eat without distraction, drink water consciously, take a shower with complete attention, drive, sit, check my work—all with undivided and full attention. I set myself up for being fully present during work conversations. I close everything, keep the phone out of sight and focus only on the person and make sure I don't drift off. I do this for meetings as well. I pay attention to my thoughts and stop judging and complaining in my head. When I am with kids, I put my phone away and really let down my guard and play and be crazy.

8. **Nutrition and hydration challenge**: I put good things into my system—drink 3 litres of water a day and snack healthy. I keep water within an arm's reach, and all unhealthy snacks are hidden away.

9. **Better-me challenge**: I appreciate at least one person for one thing every day. I communicate more, reaching out to people myself. I catch myself getting triggered and correct emotional outbursts, if any. When occasionally triggered, I breathe, go out, shake the body, or do some tapping. I also keep checking on my behaviours to ensure that they don't contradict my character or value preferences.

10. **Work-day shutdown ritual**: I set a time to end my workday and stick to that. I review the day—look at my closures, results, and outcomes for the day—and identify what worked and what didn't, and why. I clear my space, appreciate, and reward myself and create a rough plan for the next day.

11. **Purpose quest**: Every day, I do something that makes me come alive. These are not things just to entertain, but something that engages my skills to make a difference or to create something. I coach, speak, write, and read on self-development with the intent to be of service to others.

12. **De-clutter challenge**: I physically clear my space both at home and at work by organizing and arranging things around me. I clear my digital spaces often. I use incense at home to clear the stagnant air around me, use aromas to keep me focused,

and play music for concentration. I constantly try to keep the garbage out—news, thoughts, and bad behaviours.

That sounds like a lot, right? Trust me, it didn't come easy. I fell off the plan many times. So much so that I almost gave up. But with small hacks, I was able to build my way up to where I am today. Here are a few things that helped me:

- **Time audit**: Did you know you could be wasting days every year just scrolling mindlessly through social media? To make time for new, desirable things, you need to figure out your timewasters and reduce them.

- **Tiny changes**: Don't go all out at once. No one can run a marathon on their first day of running. Take time, start small, and make minute changes that will go a long way.

- **Habit linking**: This is a way to trick your mind by linking a new habit with an already ingrained pattern. For example, bathing in the morning is a pattern. If you want to start practising mirror work, you can link it to right after your bath when you are getting ready. Over time, practising mirror work in the morning will become a new habit.

- **Visible reminders**: Keep your goals in your line of sight. Using reminder cards, vision boards, and totems placed strategically can help you stick to the plan. For example, a note on the mirror about practising mirror work will serve as a reminder.

- **Build accountability**: At times, all of us need someone to push us. Having accountability partners can keep you on track when you feel demotivated or are falling off your path. I find that making public declarations of your intentions also serves this purpose.

- **Aim for quick wins**: Instead of 21-day (or longer) habit creation challenges, start with one-week challenges, and take up one thing at a time.

- **Get a coach**: Let's face it, everyone needs a coach. Coaches help you structure and streamline the whole process and keep you on track with periodic reviews. They help you understand and overcome roadblocks, and keep you focused. I have been helped in my quests by my coach, and now I coach people on achieving their lasting happiness.

- **Engaging with a like-minded tribe**: Being surrounded by people who have similar intentions and goals helps, too. One can find common ground and encouragement with a like-minded tribe. You can be a part of the Happiness Habits tribe here: *www.facebook.com/buildhappinesshabits*

'Aren't you forgetting something,' came Sid's voice. 'The most important thing while you adopt practices that serve you best in creating happiness habits is to keep asking yourself—Why am I doing all this? And the answer, "for your own peace and happiness", will keep you going.'

Well, the voice of your consciousness knows best, right?

Dealing with demotivation

> *'One of your most important tasks is to find what inspires you and use it to your advantage when you feel like giving up.'*
>
> – Unknown

There will be points in your quest that you will slip up, no matter how hard you try. But over time, you will come to realize that imperfection is an intrinsic human trait and what really matters is progress and an upward trajectory. The important thing when you are feeling demotivated is to catch yourself before you go into a downward spiral and to pull yourself back up again.

Remember, action is what will move you forward, and it's important to sustain that action.

Final actions and success markers

Each of you will start your journey to happiness from a different point. Now that you know what the seven quests entail, take some time to figure out where you are on each of these quests and what is important to you at this stage of life. For each quest, choose a level you want to improve to in the immediate future. Know that a perfect 10 is not an ideal target when you are starting off.

When you know where you are and where you want to get to, it is important to identify some success markers—indicators that tell you that you are on the right path. Success markers are, basically, a leaner version of goals that track and indicate positive progress rather than the ultimate outcome. Think of them as milestones on the road to your ultimate destination. These milestones indicate that you are making progress in the right direction, and help you stay motivated.

For example, punctuality is something I struggle with. I make my fitness trainer wait almost every day—something that I don't feel good about. I included this as a marker on my 'Better Me' quest, listing that, 'This month, I will not keep my trainer waiting for more than five minutes.' And I checked this marker periodically—am I doing great? Am I okay? Have I not changed at all? Success markers like these keep you going and help you re-strategize quickly if you are going off track.

Some examples of success markers could be:

- In the next three months, I am going to reduce my negative reaction to triggers.
- I won't watch television on weekdays.
- I will forego dessert after my main meal for a week.
- I will reduce my weight by 2 kg this month.

The idea is to have ways to track positive progress in a meaningful way and focus on smaller changes. Focusing on one ultimate goal can sometimes get too overwhelming, and then you give up entirely.

The exercises and reflections in this book and your online Happiness Habits bundle will help you compare your current state with your success markers to identify gaps. The idea is to make a plan of action to bridge these gaps and move to the next level in your quest. A good idea for the plan is to choose 12 daily rituals skewed towards your immediate priority. When you are planning for happiness, remember there will be hurdles and failures—so, plan for them too.

Implement your routine, improve, make it a habit, track progress, celebrate even small successes, reward yourself, and don't look for perfection, just progress. Over time, deepen the quests. Keep recalibrating who you are and identify newer success markers to move you to a higher level.

Keep playing the game!

REFLECTION TIME

DISCOVER

It's time to revisit your why. Ask yourself, *'what do I really want? How is this change going to help me?'*

_____

_____

_____

What are the behaviours I need to address to achieve this goal?

_____

_____

_____

What are some of the key habits I can link new ones to?

_____

_____

_____

How can I track my progress?

_____

_____

_____

What are some of the things I will do to reward myself?

_____

_____

_____

DECIDE

Make your own happiness habit plan. Write down some actions that you will do every day for each of the quests. Start small, be consistent, track your progress, have an accountability model, and celebrate your small wins.

Quest	Morning	During the Day	End of day
Better Me			
Purpose			
Balanced Life			
Emotional Mastery			
Living with Flow			
Healing			
Mindfulness			

STRATEGIZE

Download the '*Habit Tracker*' from the Happiness Habits bundle and use it to keep track of your habits.

List down what are the challenges you will face in making these a habit and what are some things that can help you stick to these habits:

Habit	What could hinder me?	What can I do to make it stick?

Use the *Quest Tracker* as demonstrated by the figure below to keep moving forward. A downloadable spreadsheet is available on your Happiness Habits bundle online.

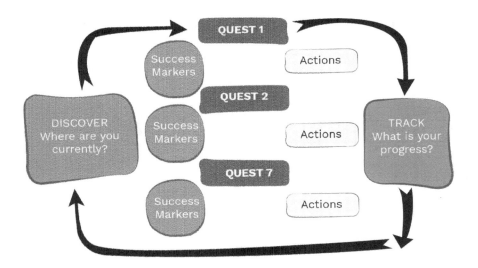

Take it to Bliss

This is the start. This is not the end. This is all meant to start you off on that path. But when you are committed to the parts, then more doors open for you, the ones that you need. These lead you to the deeper interventions that you need to reach a state of Consistent Happiness.

These are all things that are meant to pull you up a few steps from where you are.

If you have a ladder that leads to your goals at the top, what we are trying to do is to push you, goad you, to pull you up, and to make you interested in starting the climb, maybe about 4–5 steps, so that you shift from where you are now to a much better space.

By practising these Happiness Habits, you will certainly notice quite a lot of shifts in your internal states, and your external things. And, in general, there will be a lot more positive energy in your life.

Your approach towards life, your equation, becomes more positive than negative.

This is what this book does. It doesn't guarantee you everlasting happiness. It introduces you to how you will discover your purpose and pursue it.

But the fact remains that there are things that you have to do to live that purpose. And as you live that purpose, you will encounter more challenges and, at those times, there will be more things that you need to work on and keep evolving.

When we are talking of 'taking it to bliss', we are really saying that there is a much longer, deeper journey that is ahead of you. Where you are is nowhere close to where you need to be.

We've tried to get you 50 percent higher than where you were, which perhaps is enough for a lifetime, because most people don't even make that effort and get to do what we're asking you to do.

But if you are a person who says, 'No, I've already reached that 50 percent, and I'm looking for something more...' then the answer is that there is a much deeper journey that needs to be undertaken and that specific aspect or area that you need to work on, will reveal itself through the existing quests.

By doing these quests, you will progress, and you will also discover more things to work on.

And those things to work on may require you to just do these practices at a much deeper level or at a more consistent level or do something more than what is here.

For example, take meditation as a concept. Right now, you're starting with a 10-minute meditation. Move it up to 20 minutes.

Meditation, ideally, is recommended as per your age, so the older you are, the longer time you need to spend on it,

And as you deepen these practices, there is a nuance that comes up, which then tells you if you need to do something different. That's the place you want to be able to get to.

Many people say, 'oh, this is not a fun race. I have finished lap one. Now I need to end this, and I need to know all the answers to this.' You will not get that. This is not meant to be that way. And given that all these are also interlinked, which is why these quests are extremely critical for you to do as a circular thing, and not focus on one area.

If you focus on one area and you ignore the other, the latter one will create a problem.

The quests help you solve the problem, the issues that you have.

When you want to take it to bliss, you are not trying to solve problems. You are trying to enhance your practices. Say, if I've been mindful in a certain set of things, how do I become mindful in more things? How do I become mindful in everything?

That's the real journey that we are talking about—that will not come with these quests. These quests are still baby steps. These are still probably your initial things. It will get you better, but if you're really looking for the next step, the healing has to be deeper. If you want to be mindful in everything that you do, it requires you to be at a different level of awareness, different level of work. But the path is still the same; that is, **you have to work on yourself**. You have to work on yourself much deeper.

I'm still on that path. I don't think I can claim that I have reached where I need to be. But I know certain things which need to be done to get me there. I am aware of the way; I just haven't put in the work.

Waking up

And as I was reflecting on the work I had yet to put in, Sid's voice piped up.

'You know, you should stop taking this happiness thing so seriously. Life and happiness don't have to be so serious, really.'

'But it looks like there is so much yet to be explored,' I countered.

'And it'll come to you when it's time for it to show up,' Sid admonished. 'You need to chill. Think of life as a game, and just play it well, by these quests you've defined. And remember, there will always be scope to level up. It isn't like a race with a finish line—it's just progress.'

'But there must be some end to it, right?' I asked.

'Well,' Sid smiled, 'you can say there is an end, but it's not something everyone gets in one lifetime.'

'And why not?' I asked, 'What's so complicated about this end?'

'It's not complicated,' Sid's smile only got wider. 'It's the simplest thing in the Universe. The end is when your soul reaches enlightenment. When it realizes that it is the divine. But that realization needs work—many, many lifetimes even. Every time your soul is reborn, it moves closer to that realization. The game of life teaches it the lessons it needs to learn. It sheds the layers of ignorance and moves towards God-like aspects. What you can do is accelerate that journey by following the seven quests and mastering them.'

'So,' Sid continued, 'right now, just pursue your purpose, work on your character to become a better you, master your emotions, manage your energies, focus on all the important aspects of your life with a sense of balance, keep healing yourself, and strengthen your mindfulness muscle. These are the things that will help you be happy NOW. You will carry these learnings forward into your future challenges and that's all that matters at this point—you just have this moment—your full presence in this moment is what is needed. Choose to be happy in this moment.'

'That's profound! But I still have questions,' I said.

'Don't we all want to know everything,' Sid flapped his wings, ready to take flight. 'First, process what we have talked about, embody these lessons, and know that when you really need more, I will come to speak to you again. For now, let me leave you to do the heavy lifting on this eternal journey of progress. Remember to enjoy the ride. Time to wake up, buddy.'

About the Author

SRIRAM S

Sriram is a happiness coach, mentor, and author of *Happiness Habits: The Urban Professional's Guide to Good Living.*

In his two decades plus of professional experience in leading Human Resource teams across sectors and companies, Sriram realized the plight of the urban working professional. Being a teacher–trainer–mentor and a LEAP (Personal Productivity & High Performance) Expert gave him unique insights in the psyche of working professionals today—their thoughts, beliefs, and challenges.

To serve them better and help them live a happier life, Sriram went on to do several courses. He has a Coaching Skills Certification, NLP Certification, Personal Leadership & Success Certification by Emeritus & Tuck School of Business, Train the Trainer Certification by Harv Eker, Unconscious Bias Trainer Certification by ILM, Happiness Coach Certification by Berkeley Institute of Well Being.